INAUGURATE YOURSELF

INAUGURATE YOURSELF

Parvat Singh

PARTRIDGE
A Penguin Random House Company

To order additional copies of this book, contact
Partridge India
000 800 10062 62
orders.india@partridgepublishing.com

www.partridgepublishing.com/india

Contents

DEDICATED TO...

YOU – that is to all those friends, who wish to be successful prosperous and complete and who want to share this vast fund of knowledge and power of theirs amongst one another.

The Object Behind The Work...

Along with our material progress, it is equally important that our life becomes stress-free and free of perversions and at the same time there may be an enhancement in our life's happiness, peace and prosperity.

For this it is essential that you may INAUGURATE YOURSELF... and may enrich your life with love, compassion and joy, remaining committed, at the same time to your mission.

By doing so, you will be keeping yourself committed to your life's mission aimed at making your life worthwhile, meaningful and happy.

This book, I am sure, will prove of immense help in realisation of your goals in life.

With affectionate regards and best wishes

Parvat Singh
67, Ashok Vihar
Shikargarh Road, Shikargarh
Jodhpur - 342001 (Rajasthan) India
Cell : +919799884627, +91935294667
E-mail : parvatsingh48@yahoo.in

From the innermost depth of my heart...

Whenever I reflect over life, the following poem spontaneously bursts out from the innermost depths of my heart... I dedicate it to my reverend mother.

Often I wonder-
Had we not taken birth...
would we have become human beings!
Then I imagine
had we not become human beings...
would have we been
blessed with success!
And then I ponder
had we not been blessed
with this phenomenon
called life...
would we have been
anything at all!
Then comes the realisation that
if there would not have
been that miracle
called – 'Mother'...
How would have we come to
be born!

Dear friends... Mother is great – greater than greatness itself. Our parents blessings be ever with we children. – *This is what my prayer is.*

Translator's Note

When Mr. Parvat Singh gave this Hindi-to-English Translation assignment to me a few months back. I assured him of two important things – No. 1, that in my hands the translation would not be allowed to lapse into a dull and drab 'mechanical' recreation of the original text, and No. 2, it won't lack in 'communicability' in any sense of the term 'communication'.

Today having completed the assignment I dare say that I have fully lived up to my promise. God's blessings that I have been able to give the translated version creative flavour and have, at the same time have lent the colour of the readability of a very high order. And in this sense it has been quite a satisfying academic experience for me.

Let me here share with the readers the important point that Translating into other language is not just translating mechanically words. It involves doing much more. The translator is supposed to bring out the 'spirit', the emotion, the mood of the original text, the shades of the words and often their 'unsaid' part too, plus he has to 'retain the diction and idiom of the original script. Last but not the least he has to keep stuck to the subject-matter or the contents – It is all these niceties that go to make what is called a 'creative' exercise. However, for the reader what is important is the 'readability' of the translated version, and here I may repeat it that the version translated by me will not be found wanting in 'readability' at any stage.

If the readers are able to appreciate and endorse the presence of these two features – two value-points in the English Version, – I will deem my effort to have been amply rewarded.

I cannot end this note without complimenting Mr. Parvat Singh for his enterprising spirit as reflected in this project, and Mr. Ajay Surana for his energetic cooperation all through in computer-typing of the present English Version 'Swayam Ko Udghatit Karen!'

I wish the readers of the book a happy time going through its pages feeling greatly entertained and enlightened.

N.K. MEHTA
Translator in English
37, Income Tax Colony
Paota C Road,
Jodhpur-342001 (Rajasthan) India

A word about the Translator – Mr. N.K. Mehta

Mr. N.K. Mehta of Jodhpur (Rajasthan) India is an educationist, a script-writer, writer, playwright, poet and an editor, and above all is a prolific and versatile translator who has translated (from Hindi to English and vice-versa) scores of books and countless articles, write-ups, booklets, periodicals, research papers, broachers, plays and poems. He has, to his credit, translation of and script-writing for about 140 EMRC-produced U.G.C. Distance Education Feature Films repeatedly telecast from Door Darshan Channel etc. for the student watchers the world over. He is an active writer. He lives at Jodhpur (Rajasthan) India. Contact No. 0291-2540740, 9928040740, E-mail : narendrakmehta33@gmail.com

Only that can happen that is inside you, in your own self... already

That which is inside you...in-built

It appears that we are so ignorant of our own self. We have everything present in us, inside us... in-built, and yet we keep wandering about in search of it, looking for it frantically, somewhere else. It sounds rather strange.

The truth is that we are all born with some extraordinary ability or the other and therefore certainly each of us is capable of achieving great heights in terms of success and happiness in life. I hope you believe this is correct.

'But whether I believe this or not, how does it matter? You might ask.

And the answer is: it does matter, it does matter because you cannot negate or ignore the reality, and the reality here means 'your' reality and 'your reality' here, is nothing but 'your abilities': And one must then know about or believe in one's own abilities. And if you don't know about or believe in your abilities, you are just losing them or wasting them away. And this one thing alone makes the whole difference; this one thing, thus, really matters.

The person who believes and asserts- 'oh yes, I can be successful...' obviously trusts his ability and capability himself, and for sure, comes to get connected with it.

In fact, our ability and our capability, our potential and innate talent is the basis of the origin of all our successes. The realization of this infinite ability is not difficult; it is easy. An example would make it clear.

Supposing somebody told you 'you can learn driving and can become an expert driver' and believing him you proceeded to learn driving, and in a few day's time, you became an expert driver.

Now just imagine...! How all this happened? Did it happen just by a word from somebody's mouth? or else, by somebody else's belief? Or only on somebody's pointing out at this ability and the skill of yours, that it just made its way into you? Or was it some miracle that made you sit in the car quietly, and quite unawares, you drove and became an expert driver!

No... Sir, Nothing like this happened! No miracle took place. Whatever happened had its roots in reality or actuality. Whatever happened was the reality. Whatever transpired was due to your mental readiness to learn and then to drive.

The ability to learn and drive a car was very much there inside you-already inherent in you, in born and with you. And that was the reason, sole reason, why you were able to become an expert driver.

There can be no other reason than this behind it... and if at all there is one that has caught your attention, it should be only a by-product of the earlier reason itself. It is a different matter, though, that it has come on to surface 'live' only now on account of somebody else's telling you about it. Yet this experience will be reckoned as entirely yours.

Of course... it can happen that need may be felt by us to awaken somebody, to educate him, to refine him, to train, to reward and encourage him, to inspire and to make him understand, to support and to protect and to care for him.

But again, all this would be possible only if and when the person himself is ready and willing to say that... 'yes, I can do this', for, ultimately, it is the ability, the potential, the capabilities that are there inside a person, that alone can find an awakening and expression.

This brings to light the truth that – only that can happen that is inside you, in your own self... already.

Whether we own up our native competence – our ability and capability – or not, whether we recognise its presence inside or not, it is nevertheless, very much there inside us, which is its rightful place, and where it belongs. It has been present there always and it shall ever remain present there.

This original inherent competence is the best proof of the fact of our 'own' existence, our own identity, our very being itself. This competence can be solely owned by the person himself. Nobody else can be the owner thereof, nor does it recognise anybody else's right over it. Any one of us, whenever we like can get connected to it, get to be 'one' with it and become successful, prosperous, and an enriching and enriched personality.

We can understand this thing even consciously – For instance, does sugar need to demonstrate that it is sweet? –No, it does not! The reason is simple. The reason is that sweetness is its reality, its quintessence, its attribute. We may taste sugar any number of times, it will taste sweet. Sweetness is its characteristic quality, its typical property. This quality is ever present in it. In fact, it is its very nature, very temperament.

Again this sugar may drop down on the floor, it may get crushed or may get scattered and grinded or mixed, still it does not lose its essential attribute, that is... sweetness. The same is true of our abilities and capabilities which are ever present inside us. Relying on them we can turn every event of our life into a grand success.

In fact, what truth or the reality needs is not any proof or testimony, what it needs is 'faith'. As soon as the faith in yourself is restored, the truth or the reality will come to appear, come to the fore, of its own accord.

What do you say – did Michael Schumacher become a Formula–1 Champion by virtue of somebody else's ability? –Certainly not. The truth is that Formula–1 Championship was already there in his very nature, in his very temper, in his veins and in his very blood. It was his unimpeachable faith and confidence in his own ability that was the one single reason why he got success in his venture.

Again, the celebrated Space traveller Sunita Williams while embarking on her 'mission Discovery' had said in her message – if you have faith in yourself, your *dreams are realized.* And lo...! The result of this faith, this confidence turned out so right in that, she had already broken the record of staying in the space the longest, as she was getting ready to land on the Earth.

The entire world was eager to accord welcome to her on the Earth to the thundering of the never-ending applause to rejoice the occasion. All her friends and colleagues at NASA had put on red dress in her honour, as this particular day had got itself registered in the human memory and on the pages of world history as the 'Sunita William's Day'. Simply incredible, simply wonderful – this thrust of trust. Here is a classical example of the fact that the thrust of trust in your mission, and trust or confidence in your own self – can work wonders!

Laxmi N. Mittal was always utterly confident of his own managerial ability as he had bought a Company running in losses, and by the sheer dint of his managerial acumen, made the pendulum of this Company swing back to the side of profits. Today his steel-production business empire knows no stopping in terms of its growth. Record production and distribution have made him the unquestioned Emperor of the Steel business empire. In the course of his lecture at IOC Jaipur, he said, –'When I went to Indonesia, nobody would believe that

I could produce *steel* there. But if you possess firm determination and faith in yourself, nothing can stop you from attaining what you want to attain'. And today it is common knowledge that, the Steel King, Laxmi N Mittal is one of the world's richest persons.

Hundreds of such success-stories happening around us only go to point out to one moral, namely, that one who has faith in himself, comes to acquire his abilities and capabilities, automatically. And therefore, we have reason to conclude that our faith in ourselves in today's context is the biggest asset and hence a challenge for us.

Friends, unless and until we are able to liberate ourselves from the ever-growing shadows of the dark forces of crises and conflicts, doubts and suspicion 'in-side' us, we will refuse to accept our own successes despite their apparent readiness to shoot-forth.

In other words, as soon as our inner self, our mind, gets rid of the aforesaid conflicts and doubts... our thoughts of success would automatically find their way into our heart and mind and occupy the same like the landlord of a place occupying his own house in his own right.

Let us see what Lata Mangeskhar, the music Queen of India, has to say in this regard: 'It is not the outside influences that made me a singer. Music and abundance of it, it was already there in me. Music pervades my very being.'

Success is not a mere coincidence – it is the end-product of a deliberate, continuous exercise of your own choice of picking out your abilities

By virtue of being a sensitive creature, we are prone to entertain new ideas knocking at our mind's doors. These new ideas are the result of our everyday experiences – of what we see, hear, learn, understand, experience and feel from things and happenings around us. An endless and continuous chain of thoughts runs like an undercurrent inside us all the time. It is due to this rare gift of the powers of thinking given to us by Nature that we are the supreme - most amongst all the creatures of this planet today.

Again it is due to this power of thinking that wisdom and a sense of power emerges from inside us. Not only this, we posses yet another wonderful feature and that is discretion..., by exercising which we are able to analyse the thoughts and ideas rising in our minds and sift the grain of good, healthy, positive and pure ideas from the chaff of the bad, unhealthy, negative and evil ideas from our minds. Thus we are able to address ourselves to good thoughts.

Whatever progress and development has taken place in the world it is, by and large, the product of the thoughts and thought processes of the successful and great minds of the world. That's why anybody from us can pay attention to these thoughts and can apprehend and adopt them, and make them a part of his own character, personality and success.

The real beginning of success and prosperity takes place with the entertaining of a good feeling about our own selves... A good feeling about own self does not necessarily mean 'ego' or 'false pride'; it is, instead, that healthy state of mind... which inspires you and encourages you to separate the right and meaningful thoughts from a whole lot of a mass of other kind of thoughts encased in your mind. Albeit the ego is wherein you refuse to admit your own authenticity (due to your own perception of modesty).

As a matter of fact you come to become what you really think or take yourself to be. And you become what you come to do or come to be doing. Whatever you elect to be you submit yourself to the role in to it, you almost come to surrender yourself to it, and you get belonged to it. Your life starts taking a shape in terms of the direction in which you have started proceeding. If there is anybody who happens to stand between your thoughts and you, it is none else, it is you... yourself alone.

Because whatever has been going on or goes on, its first information reaches you alone. Your sensibilities have the first direct contact with your mind. The first information report of the possible direction of your life is lodged with you... yourself alone. Your interest, preferences etc. are best known to you. That is, if there is any one closest to your selection, it is none else than you alone.

All these things prove that it is you who should select your 'success' yourself using your own 'discretion'... because your success is not just a matter of coincidence, it is the outcome of your own conscious selection and is a continuous exercise...

In fact, the need to select coincidences never arises. They are already there, available, in our nature itself. It is the kind of selection you proceed with, determines that the kind of coincidences (you want). As you select so will you confront the coincidences.

Knowing all this... you must understand the importance of your very being, your existence, your identity. Understand the importance of your life too.

Understand the importance of your abilities and capabilities, understand the importance of your own precious, valuable thoughts. Think of the importance of your own belief. Realise the importance of a 'change' in your own self and be your own master.

Why is this so?... It is because it is in your nature to get belonged to whatever you feel is important.

That's why instead of looking this side and that side, when we look to our own thoughts with attention, our task becomes easy. We are able to understand as to what we are to do and what not to do. The reason is that attention – 'due' attention – 'good' attention-helps us to have the knowledge and power to understand meaningful thoughts as well as meaningless ones. In this way we are able to abandon the evil and apprehend the good.

We can do so when we are free of tension and are free in mind. Whatever selection we make or choice we exercise in this situation it is, so to say, unmixed and devoid of any perversions. This unmixed, pure thought is the quintessence, the crux, the substance of the matter. Such a thought is bound to be successful.

While, after the school hours, other children would loiter around, Shri Shri Ravi Shankar, the boy, would sit in meditation for hours together so that he might develop the 'art of living'. The result is before us – today his courses (The Art of Living) are being run all over the world and lacs of our friends and people are taking lessons on them and getting instructed in the said art.

When I was in class X, one of my teacher, Gopidasji had decided that he would open a school, I fully remember that he used to say 'I wish to open a school where people would not only get education but will also learn how to lead an independent and self-sustained life.' Triggered with this idea, he began to put his steps forwards on to his goal. And lo...! The Vijai Adarsh Vidya Mandir has come out today as a well-known institution of the city.

After a few years when I called on him to congratulate and compliment him on this great achievement the realisation of this dream of his – his very short but profound answer was – 'This is just a beginning...'

What I feel is that everybody wants to become successful, but only rather superficially, only outwardly. This is the reason why our friends make a selection of the success easily, but when it comes to carrying it out with firm resolve and due determination, they just usually pull themselves back. By doing this, they are thrown back to lead and pass on an exhausted existence, a tired life, a nameless, faceless, anonymous life, despite having all the abilities and potential inside them.

The selection or exercising choice of success is as important, essential and imperative, as its execution or implementation is. The firm resolves to carrying it out, results in the necessary firmness or determination of thoughts too.

To be successful now, is a resolve taken by you...

As soon as our selection of the ideas relating to success is finalised we at once, come to decide saying – 'Oh yes, I have to make this idea a success at any cost, we vow to ourselves – 'Oh yes, come whatever, I have to turn this idea into a success-story. And along with the resolve, our selection itself turns into a firm resolve. After this, there is no going back, indeed. And we get to get mentally ready with all the might at our command and our abilities and potentialities come to get collected, mustering their strength and become active in this area of ideas.

Nothing of course, now, can stop us from proceeding further in our plan. Thinking so, we mentally reach a stage where success seems so very within our reach – a point where we had so dearly wished arriving at.

The question now arises, can you be trustworthy to your own self at every stage of the selection of ideas relating to success? Can you maintain your trust, your confidence in yourself, even after having attained the highest point, the pinnacle, the zenith of your success? It is a big question, but its answer, too, is with you and with nobody else. If your answer is 'yes', then your statement is as trustworthy as the sun is to the morning and as easy, natural and obvious as breathing is to our body.

But if you choose to say 'no', the proposition becomes equally non-feasible, hard and difficult, being full of complications. Of course the breath will go on even then. Yes, it won't stop. In life, nothing stops. And then in the same vein, I am inclined to say 'nothing is impossible', everything is in your hand – yes and no – either of them, the decision is to be taken by you.. only. You are free to take a decision presently at your will!

Always remember – To be successful now is a resolve taken by you.

Yes, a firm resolve... nothing less than it, nothing more. Nothing after it, nothing before. Nothing to left of it, nothing to right. Nothing above it, nothing below. Just one single decision, one firm resolve, an infallible and a complete decision. And it is urged that you have to stick to it, and work for it doggedly.

And so the moment you do not adhere strictly to this decision, you are again in a new situation demanding yet another new selection.

The important question here is – why do we always wish to keep our faith up? The answer is credibility. The moment we lose our faith we break our contact with the reality. That is why, I repeat, we always try to, sustain our faith at all costs. As soon the faith comes into play, prosperity, happiness and peace begins to show themselves up.

Faith gives energy to our native capabilities and the goal lends it the necessary momentum...

The supreme Joy alone is the supreme objective for all of us

I have never met a person who has ever said that I don't want to be happy. Have you ever met such a person? Perhaps not...! and even if there were someone to say like that, be sure he is telling a lie.

We all are human beings, We all the time, since our birth, have been busy pursuing the goal of attaining pleasure or happiness. This makes it clear that to be happy is a prime need of ours. We must admit forthwith this reality of our day-to-day life.

This whole world, today exists on account of our needs, stable or changing, inert or dynamic, changing or changeable depending upon the circumstances. Need is the only basis, the basic motivator which makes us do or not do certain things. Just as moving of an electric fan may be a necessity on one occasion and not to move may also be a necessity at some other.

Had it, not been so, we would never have been motivated to do things. We would never have cared to get up, nor would have walked, eaten, drunk, breathed and even would not have taken birth...!

May be someone might say – 'I do not need anything, I have no needs of my own'. Even this might be interpreted to mean that the fellow keeps his needs to be the minimum.

So this man feels pleased even when he has got bare minimum things with him. That brings us back to the point that at the bottom of every goal or objective, the element of 'being pleased' is always very much there. Or let us put it like this, that to feel pleased, to have pleasure, to feel happy is the principal aim or objective behind all our actions, behind whatever we do.

When we come to recognise our needs, those the special needs come to become our aim, our objective, our target, our goal.

Come on, let's discuss this point here right now – supposing you asked as to what your aim in life is? – each one of us will have different answers to give – our answer could be – I wish to earn a lot of money – I want to become a player – I wish to be a businessman – I wish to be a singer – I wish to be a leader – I wish to be a writer – I wish to earn name and fame – I want to serve – I want to love – and so on and so forth. Thus people want to become scientists, engineers, doctors, actors, educationists technicians, army men, foremen etc etc. That is, we all want to become something, want to be successful in our work and aim.

If the next obvious question in this chain is put. It would be – Why do you want to be successful? What do you want to achieve at the end of the day? The obvious answer would be – 'so that I can attain prosperity and happiness, joy and peace'. In other words, we wish to be happy and full of joy every moment of our life. In other words, it is the desire for joy and happiness that is the motivating factor behind our active life that we are leading at present.

In fine, what becomes as clear as crystal, is that attainment of supreme joy is the supreme objective of each one of we people of this planet.

We might study and understand all the definitions of success but the quintessence of all of them would be that success lies in happiness, joy and pleasure, which are attributes of success.

If it be so, then the question arises; why can't we remain happy through every moment – why can't we all of a sudden fulfil all our wishes. The answer to this 'why' is : forgetting – that is, to forget. What we consciously keep in mind, becomes a part of our nature, and what we forget, tends to quit our mind. To bring it back into our nature, we have to keep practising for it until the time it gets retrieved to our temperament permanently. Thus, what is in-built in us as a part of our temperament, goes on happening and happening.

Success, in fact, is an event and to be successful is instinct – our instinctive nature. In other words, to succeed is to be successful in every big or small event of our life. This success, in turn, leaves a good feeling in our body and mind so that every moment becomes joyous, musical, sweet, happy and pleasurable and delightful, every day becomes a festive day and by being aware of our basic craze and desire for success, we can achieve even big things, big heights.

We can attain big successes by rendering them into small fragments of objectives. We shall talk about this aspect in detail in the chapters that follows in this book.

What pains me is the fact that many a friends of ours are often seen going off the track of their basic instinct of success and take to other ways or run after other things strayed away from their main path. They go against their very nature and get eluded by false dreams into meaningless pursuits. They start running after illusions, after shadows rather than substances. That is why despite being talented, and having a potential, success stays away from them leaving them to suffer in misery, tension, stress, and pain and in doubt and disillusionment.

Thoughtful and farsighted people look to permanent and long term advantages. That's why they believe in the fulfillment of needs of others as a means of fulfillment of 'their' success. Even Nature is seen to be proving helpful in these ventures of theirs. They feel and believe that if others prosper, it would automatically include their welfare and prosperity also... And this is what success is all about. Such people believe in the achievement of objectives not for their own selfish ends, but as an opportunity to serve others as well, more.

Therefore if one has in mind any ideas or new ideas about success, one must put them into action, otherwise it (the idea) would either vanish as fast as it came, or it would get stuck up at the same place where it originally was. Therefore, translating an idea into action is a principle that should be given top-priority by you. If you do so, you could become successful in life, and could contribute to the society too, at the same time.

In still other words, a great man is not he who looks to successful ideas or who dreams success dreams, but one who proceeds to turn them into success by means of prompt and appropriate action.

The interesting thing about success is that the 'seat' of success remains always empty, and as such anyone who wants to occupy it can do so and ride it smooth on the road to his goal and enjoy it too. Then what should you wait for... why not occupy it – *It is still empty...!*

Come on dear readers, then employ your ability and capability, your talent and your potential into practice, so that you may translate the dreams you are nurturing in your mind at present, into reality, and thereby enhance the feeling of delight experienced as a sequel to success that rightfully follows the realisation of the dreams...

Substance...

Pay attention to the following points :-

- In order to know my own self thoroughly I shall keep practicing self-introspection.
- The bases of my creations are none but my own inner abilities and capabilities. Realising this, I shall repose my trust in my own potentialities that are innate to me. I shall always accept this reality and on the basis of this reality I shall devote myself fully to the field of work in my quest for success.
- The innate potentialities had already been present there in me, it is present even today and it will ever be a part of me in future too. The native potential is but the justification of my own identity or existence.
- I shall keep being unmindful of the internal conflicts, doubts and suspicions coming in the way, and shall, in all events, keep myself alive and kicking in the field of my creations and successes.
- I shall always see to my thoughts with a discerning eye and shall keep making due selections of the constructive ideas continuously.
- I shall always entertain a good feeling about my own self and thus nursing better thoughts in my mind, shall make my life better.
- In respect of my work, I shall certainly keep my eyes open all round and learn things therefrom, but my decisions will be my own and in the decision-making, I shall be my own master.
- The resolve made or the decision taken by me, shall be stuck to in its entirety in letter as well as in spirit.
- I shall keep my conduct in consonance with the laws of Nature. This will help me gather happy coincidences and thereby shall make my path to success easier.
- I shall participate in other people's successes also and shall thereby enhance the grace of my own hard-earned success.
- The first and the foremost goal of my active life shall be to attain happiness and by connecting it with success I shall be able to realise my dream.

Time Limit Passes off...
but Time ever remains

Time is the same for everyone –

'I wish to do so many things – They are all due since long – but what to do ... just don't find time enough for those things... I am not able to get over the this-&-that's of everyday life', Thus complained one of my acquaintances who appeared to be rather sore about paucity of time.

'Now, Time – it is the same to everyone. It is equally at the disposal of both successful people as well as those who are not so successful. Time from its own side does no injustice – all are equal in the eye of Time. It is not the case that those who work more get some extra 'time' for their use'. I tried to reason with him.

'Of course, I do understand it, but still you know – worldly and material obligations', spoke he with a deep sigh –'Oh, things are not that easy...!'

Now just, take a pause to think... Is time really such a big problem with most of our friends? Had this been correct, then could many of the ordinary mortals amongst us have really become great men. Indeed not...! Which means that 'time' is the same in quantum for them as well as for us.

Time at the disposal of Mahatma Gandhi was equally the same in quantum as it is with us or was at the disposal of Abraham Lincoln, Helen Keller and of Bill Gates as it is with us. That is, it is there full 24 hours, full 30 days and full so many years, and the whole life as such. Time is there – very much there with us, all through our lifetime, whether one is a big man or an ordinary man, it hardly matters.

The problem, however, is that while most of our friends think that they have no time, but they do not know as to where and how they are making use of the time they are having. This is due to this thoughtlessness or want of understanding that they are employing right time in wrong things, wrong pursuits.

Wasting time was only one meaning – to waste away life

If we peep into our life, we would find how and in what manner are we wasting our precious time. I have drawn up a list in this respect, which I may say is not exhaustive, but never the less it is quite suggestive:-

- In keeping our important things here and there, and then in looking for them when the need arises.
- To stand in a queue for completing our work and then waiting for our turn.
- By indulging in discussing politics, games and sports, films, social issues and individuals, at random and needlessly.
- In taking to excessive drinking, gambling and taking to deadly drugs in the name of just 'having fun' or having 'a gala time'.
- In watching obscene films, TV programmes and Ads of very cheap quality and the ones having adverse moral undertones (morally degrading effects on us).
- To relax when it is really time for work, and to work, when it is time to relax.
- In reading sensational news, obscene books and dirty literature.
- In unnecessarily scolding the children around, in unwantedly interfering in the neighbour's matters, unnecessarily and or humiliating the old people around.
- In listening to the lectures seeking to mislead the people and create controversies.
- In gossip-mongering, in making false critical comments, in blowing your own trumpet, in frivolous and loose talk, in hypocritical showing off and in vain actions and behaviour.
- In making mockery of the people, making fun of others in humiliating them by oblique remarks, or satirical comments.
- To tell a lie to hide a lie, and to tell a hundred another lies in order to hide untruth.
- Unwarranted and unwanted lecturing to others and then to bear the consequences in the shape of strained relations.
- Falling ill by adopting an unnatural life style and then in ridding yourself of the diseases caused as the result of faulty living.

- In squandering or wasting away the hard earned money and then to take to additional burden of earning extra bucks.
- In buying or collecting unwanted articles of facility and then arranging for additional resources for user, maintenance and conservation or repairs thereof.
- To giving uninvited advice to others repeatedly and then in insisting upon them to follow the advice.
- In doing things that need not be done, in putting off the more important tasks and then to suffer the consequences thereof.
- To listen to annoyingly loud music and then in watching the provokingly stimulating gestures caused by the said blasting music.
- In witnessing fights and quarrels and also in adding fuel to the fire.
- In taking endlessly on mobile phone, on reading dirty and cheap messages thereon, and in sharing the said messages and also in creating your own messages.
- Wrong indiscreet use of the internet.
- In causing rubbish to spread in the office or at home and then to try to remove it and thrown it outside.
- In making unnecessary complaints.
- In extending or offering to extend uninvited cooperation to some other person and causing harassment to them in the process.
- In committing thefts or dacoity or murder or to indulge in hooliganism, rioting and spreading terror and then to attempt to dupe the law or to evade it, and in absconding and then in serving the sentence after being caught and traced and convicted.
- In hurting the egos of one another.
- In aiding strikes with a view to promoting your own vested interest and leading a particular group in a strike etc with an eye on leadership.
- In practicing wrong traditions, wrong beliefs and hollow rituals.
- In indulging in excessive sleeping and eating.
- In subjecting animals and birds to cruelty, harassment and in taking away their liberty and in indulging in killing them.
- To intrude upon the personal lives of others and to form wrong opinion about them.
- To pass leisure time doing nothing.

- To pursue superstition and blind belief and then to lament over the adverse results.
- In working for uncertain targets and to suffer the consequences later on.
- In getting their work expedited and in-stalling the other people's work, indulging thereby in encouraging toutism, bribe-giving and corruption.
- In obtaining education and training which is impractical and unemployment- enhancing.
- In not exercising our right to vote or in exercising it wrongly and then later on in accusing the administration.
- In indulging in ever-teasing and to keep and show a malicious, humiliating and harassing attitude.
- To consider the whole world foolish and to consider himself the wisest.
- To look, for everything, to others or to the government.
- To support or extend your cooperation in ideas and actions leading to encourage evils like violence, bigotism, inequality, communalism, casteism, aparthied or colour-discrimination, and bad social-customs, crimes against society etc.
- To damage or harm nature and then to suffer the resultant ill-effects.
- To lose your freedom of existence under wrongful influence of others.
- Misusing the means, the facilities the discoveries and researches and resources of energy meant for welfare, prosperity, progress and development and thereby to making his own life and others life miserable.
- To make life unnecessarily, unduly serious where it can be taken lightly.
- To stall the thoughts seeking to delights us and give us joy.

Dear readers – the above list is getting too long which implies that it is more or a list of the ways in which we are ruining ourselves rather than anything else. Although it is not our intention to hurt somebody's feelings, but its intention or purpose to make you alert with regard to your 'time' is loud and clear. It is obvious that by becoming aware of the value of 'time', we may tend to make a better and judicious use of it. Otherwise' wasting time has only one meaning – 'to waste away life.'

As we go on becoming aware of the danger of wrong use of time, we can automatically find extra time for success.

The time which unsuccessful people waste is utilised by the successful ones

The poet and philosopher Emerson says – 'Every moment of your precious time should be spent in hard work. By doing so, not a moment is left that may be resented'.

One of the ways to 'find' time is to spend some precious time with the objectives which we consider to be valuable. At the same time we may invest or spend the time in the company of those of our fellowmen who are ready and willing to understand and value our objectives and In the process, to go ahead in life. Thus the volume of our saved time increases, at every next level. This increase in the final volume of time enhances our achievements and attainments. This... in fact is what 'success' is. Instead of whiling away our time in unnecessary activities, we may better adopt this course of action.

In fact, we can always find time for the work that we really enjoy doing or what is indispensable for us, i.e. without which we cannot do anything. For instance, a singer who is always more than ready to sing, because he enjoys singing. Similarly howsoever busy we may be, we can always find time to eat and drink and breathe, for the simple reason that without these things we cannot do. Where did 'this time', then come from? We did find it because we knew we would not be able to do without it.

Exactly the same thing applies to 'Success' and the person who takes interest in achieving success, and the one who does not feel good without success for being successful, would always be able to develop ways to find time.

Therefore, success does not lie in just passing time. It lies in making good use of time.

While the whole world lay deep asleep in it beds in the night, A. R. Rehman, the magical musician, worked usually in his studios weaving ever new melodies of sound into rare musical compositions, the kind of which only he is capable of making/creating – the melodious compositions that are so touching, compositions that make inroads into the very core of our heart and of which the whole world is simply mad, mad, mad...

Prime Ministers of India and Presidents of America – Office hours over – and they languishing in their sofas in their drawing room over a cup of tea and enjoying TV scene – Do you have this kind of picture in your mind for these kinds of 'big' men like Presidents of America and Prime Ministers of India? No, you are absolutely mistaken. These big men have no time for rest or relaxation. All their time is 'Success-time', that is, 'devoted to success'. That exactly is why they are different from the lesser mortals like us. That exactly is the reason why they are Presidents or Prime Ministers of countries and are so very high ups.

All these are the examples of the fact, the thing called 'time' is put to due use by successful persons, whereas 'the same thing' (i.e. the said 'time') is just wasted by the unsuccessful people. In other words, the phenomenon called 'time' is a necessity for the successful persons, whereas it is a luxury for unsuccessful ones for they are the definite squanderers of time.

The interesting thing is that it is very easy to say that 'we have no time', but the fact is that to pass 'idle' time is a very tough exercise by itself. All the emptiness, all the monotony, the discontent or dissatisfaction or tiredness in our life is a gift of this 'idle time' often called 'leisure'. We can fill this emptiness with a gainful work.

The important thing is not that we have no time, and that are wanting in time. What is surprising is that we are not ready and prepared for the thing called 'success'. As soon as we are 'ready and willing' for success, the time for success becomes automatically available.

The 'time span' passes off but 'time' ever remains.

The want of time is advocated by such of our friends who are conscious of the uncertainty of time. That is why they look to the watch every now and then. The result is that instead of 'living' with the time at their disposal, they get entangled into its way.

Whereas our real success does not lie in its getting entangled or grappling with time, it lies in enjoying it.

We can do so if we reach this state of timelessness. In such a state, all our attention gets focused on attaining success and as such we are able to get at the wholesomeness of the holistic view of time, and in such a state and as a result, the chances of our getting success become certain.

Those who recognise the value of time, gets their own recognition assured along with the passage of time, like how Sania Mirza the renowned Tennis player, stated in an interview about her desire for success that —'in every generation, there are achievers' whom Time accords recognition.'

The time that stands passed can never come back or be retrieved at any cost, But today's working day has come again with all its freshness. The entire day, then, lies open before you like a clean slate. Yes, and therefore, you may utilise it in whatever way you like – the choice is yours, the deal is open.

Always remember this – then, that time-span passes... but Time ever remains.

The good news, as such, is that Time does not use us – it is we who use Time. The moral, then, is that we should not allow ourselves to be exploited by time – rather we ought to put it to proper use. And to know all this is to come to our senses – *to rise up to the need, to rise to the occasion!*

Come on guys, then, let's gear ourselves up. It is time for us to do so, the aim being that we become conscious of the ensuing times, and all times for us become success time or a success-story...

Substance...

Pay attention to the following points :-

- Time, or say, quantum of time makes no discrimination amongst people. It is the same in quantum for all.
- I, for one, have the same amount of time that is at the disposal of successful and great people. That is, the time with me is equal in quantum to the time that was with Mahatma Gandhi, or for that matter, with Abraham Lincoln or Hellen Keller or with Bill Gates.
- With this concept in mind, I shall try to find out as how and where? I am spending the time that is available with me.
- By being thus conscious or more aware of the time I spend, I shall avoid making a wrong use of it and shall see to it that I am aware of the need to spend it usefully and correctly.
- It is thus that I shall relate my time with success and shall thereby connect this success with my life.
- I shall be dedicating most of my time to the particular goal that is really precious to me.
- Further, I shall invest my time in those colleagues who by becoming participants of my goal wish to march forward to realise it, as also to cause their own enhancement.
- By making a right and proper use of my time, I shall add to its value in terms of it usefulness or utility.
- I shall devote all my attention to my ability to act and thus shall go all out to enjoy the fruit thereof.

By Delegating One's Responsibility One Can Not Become Free From Accountability

Often we try to shift our responsibility onto others or try to escape from it or to run away from it

Rohan and Shravan were good friends, as well as colleagues. Once Rohan came in his new shirt 'Sharwan liked it very much. He expressed his desire to have such a shirt for himself too – 'Where did you bring it from, Rohan? Can't you get one for me too?' This is how Sharwan proposed that Rohan should bring one for him too.

Rohan promised to do so. The next day, Shrawan again made a mention of the shirt. Thereupon suddenly Rohan said – 'Oh dear' I had brought the shirt already but it had got left Manish's house and therefore you might collect it from Manish's house.

Sharwan duly collected the shirt from Manish's place but only to find that the shirt was short in length. He was a little sore about it, On Sharwan's saying that he (Rohan) ought to have brought a piece of proper measurement, Rohan tried to pacify Shrawan by saying – 'No big deal, I had bought it from the National Handloom and as such you can get it changed whenever you happen to pass that side.'

Shrawan reached National Handloom so soon he got free from the office and requested the Counter-fellow to get the shirt in question changed as it was not as per his size. Thereupon the man on the counter said – 'Please show me the bill and then you can get it changed at the counter no. 4'.

But... 'bill'? now was this new problem. What to do – he thought! as the bill was with Rohan himself. A little perplexed Shrawan rang up Rohan saying complainingly – 'Yaar, you did not care to give me the Bill?'

'Oh then it should be at my house – I shall find out just now – 'On enquiring from home, the reply that came from the other side was to the effect that 'Rohan had completely forgotten about it – 'why hadn't this been told earlier? The shirt had already been washed and the 'bill' obviously had been washed off too.'

Disappointment, hopelessness, helplessness – whatever you may say, it continued and the end was not in sight!

Now let us have a peep into our own lives... Do we, too, not behave at times, like Rohan and Sharvan – Shifting the responsibility on others to avoid taking upon ourselves a responsibility or running away from it? Aren't we too made of the same stuff? – who knows this better than we ourselves!

Mutual guidance or counseling is not a bad thing, but we have to understand the difference between 'taking work from others' and discharging our own responsibility ourselves. Often we forget our own responsibility in a zeal to seeking cooperation from others.

For, every task demands our full involvement – otherwise it cannot pass as a 'perfect' task. That's why it is not a good policy to try to shift our responsibility and to expect that getting a task done by other is as good as doing it yourself. No, you cannot expect others to do your task with the same efficiency that you possess, the simple reason being that no two persons can do a job exactly in the same manner. Because no two persons can be exactly similar in their nature and work – not even twins.

If we push off work from our shoulders, complaints as regards the efficiency of its execution, will recoil on us.

Irresponsibility only entails brings in complaints

The only responsible persons for our failures are nobody else than we ourselves. The more we try to run away from the responsibilities, the farther we get from success.

The mentality or mindset we often begin to have is that somebody else may do our job and we may be spared of the trouble and may sleep tight.

We, of course, say that the Government is useless – but the million dollar question is, who has elected this wrong kind of Government? – We resent that the entire system has got rotten, but we forget as to how much we have contributed in spoiling it to this extent? – We allege that there is so much of dirt and rubbish and filth, but it is we who are also responsible for this! – We admit the corruption is going rampant, but it is we ourselves who do not refrain from giving a bribe when the need arises! We do understand that women empowerment is important and is the call of the hour, but it is we ourselves, on the other hand, that take pride in discriminating between our son and daughter! – and have a biased eye in favour of the son we go about telling people that social evils are spreading, but we ourselves do not hesitate even for a moment, in selling out our son in return of a 'big dowry'!

In short, there are a thousand things, which warn us that unless we discharge our responsibilities in right earnest and behave in a more dignified manner, the heap of our complaints will mount, in as much as irresponsibility can only multiply complaints and do nothing else.

It is futile to expect pure oxygen when we are sitting on a rather, stinking heap of rubbish and filth. If we wish to come out of this suffocation and breathe in fresh air, then there are only two options with us. First – to remove the rubbish, destroy it, and make a neat and clean atmosphere around. And second – to leave the place and walk off or tread on a new path.

But the question is a where would you go...? There is no escape – this rubbish and dirt will follow you wheresoever you go. The better way therefore, is that the dirt, the rubbish should be destroyed and destroyed completely. As soon as the filth gets destroyed, room will be automatically made for fresh air.

The real beginning of a reform takes place from nowhere else, but from your own self. Therefore, you should not bother yourself and say –'why is this so' – 'why is this not so' or that – 'for me it ought to have been like this' etc., Instead channelise your thought to the question 'what can I do from my side in order to remedy this particular wrong?' And there is the rub. As soon as you become conscious of your own responsibility, you automatically start yourself start preparing for completing the task or discharging the responsibility. This proves that to 'rouse your sense of responsibility towards yourself' is the paramount responsibility on your part.

Our real problem is not that we cannot 'be' responsible – the real difficulty is that we don't come up true to our own expectations. And the converse, therefore, is true, namely, that the moment we get to rise up to our own expectations, we become conscious for and alert towards our own responsibility. It is this alertness ('which is the enemy' of the inertness) that, really prompts us to proceed further up, on the road to adventure.

The compulsion behind discharge of our responsibilities is conscious. The realisation of responsibility – compels us to undertake the same

The prime difference between a responsible person and a not-so-responsible one is that the responsible person makes himself liable and responsible for the task, whereas' the irresponsible person will try to find somebody else on whom to cast the responsibility.

Sanjay had completed his Management course. He talked the matter of his career over to his father. His father told him that there was a certain friend of his employed with a five-star Hotel belonging to a big hotel group, and as such he would be making efforts for Sanjay's job through him. He told Sanjay that he would be talking to that friend of his right then.

Sanjay liked his father's suggestion, but despite this, he did not stop here and continued to make his own efforts simultaneously. That was a right thing to do, for to find a job, was after all his own responsibility.

And now, see... how responsibility itself works itself out. Sanjay got selected in a big group of company's newly launched Hotel. After a few days his father friend's call came and it was to the effect that a vacancy had fallen in a good hotel of his block and everything had been talked over and as such I might send Sanjay there.

For sure, there were two options open before Sanjay. It was open to him to have adopted a course that henceforth would be better for him. The reason was that although he did have consultations with others, but he had all the time kept connected himself with his basic responsibility.

Now, just imagine... had he left the task of looking for a job totally to his friend's father, and supposing for the same reason his father's friend would have failed to manage a job for him, an intriguing situation would have developed. Would it have been proper, then, to have blamed his friend's father? Certainly not!

The task which we are supposed to do, has got to be done, at all cost by ourselves alone. The same thing would ensue if there was nobody prepared to take up your responsibility. Therefore I repeat with due apologies, that we can achieve success only by being responsible, because the consciousness of being successful goads us, prompts us, motivates us, compels us to duly discharge this responsibility of ours.

Can it happen that thirsty is somebody else and it is you whose thirst gets quenched! It cannot happen that somebody else does a task and satisfaction that takes place is yours! It cannot be that the food is eaten by some other person and it is you who come to gain the energy! ... All these things are impossibilities.

It is altogether a different matter, however, that the food may be arranged by 'A' for 'B', then just the eating or chewing part of it will have to be done by 'B' alone. Again, it is possible, that you may get success due to somebody else's efforts. But then this cannot be treated as your success. The credit ought to go to him, for it is he who discharged an additional task. It would be 'a borrowed success' so far as you are concerned. You would be regarded the same as you were earlier – i.e., absolutely weak and timid.

So the moral of this entire story is that you cannot be free – i.e., you cannot escape responsibility by delegating your responsibility and passing the buck onto others.

As soon as one becomes conscious of his responsibility, his attention gets focused onto the task of fulfilling it and he becomes thereby a good deal more responsible.

Responsibility is proportionate to the right

To be successful and to be happy is our right. Therefore our interest lies in the fact that we remain conscious of this right of ours. But then to talk about one's own right is the right of that person alone who discharge fully his own responsibility. This means that a right is always attached to a responsibility and the person who discharges his responsibility duly, he would get his right without even asking for it. Would it not be so, even a right would become a burden on us.

The discharging of responsibility fully, itself amounts to your right. The more you march forward in the direction of your responsibility, the wider your area of the right becomes. In the process, the atmosphere around you helps in making your right reach you and thereby you are, able to wish to achieve. Thereby you are able to attain what you wanted to attain. And there you are! ... This is what you call your success is! ... The moral is – this is how we can turn the due discharge of our responsibility into our right.

As per a news, in the course of 16th congress in November 2002 when the Hoo Jintao the General Secretary of the Government party of China was selected President of China, he was not a popular name or figure in the outside world. But the way he discharged his Presidential duties and responsibilities, the country made such tremendous strides on all fronts, that the whole world became his ardent admirers, the admirers of the way China had become such a super-power of the world.

As we march ahead discharging our responsibilities, our internal powers get enhanced. Our energy level gets boosted up at every phase of the attainment in proportion to the success. Our consciousness of being more powerful, everyday prepares us for possibilities of assuming more responsibilities.

'We all realise it ourselves that whatever we are doing in fact is just a drop in the ocean, but if there were no drops in the ocean, the ocean would not have been the ocean'. - Mother Teresa

To develop our own self is our real responsibility

Our real responsibility lies in developing our own-self and thereby reach the pinnacle of our success. What I believe is that to take ourselves to that highest point is our, own moral responsibility. If we are able to do so. we can have the satisfaction of giving the world a very valuable gift from our side.

In fact, individuals make a family, families make a society, societies make a nation and nations go to make the whole world. If we remove the individuals from this structure, what will happen and what remains behind...? Perhaps nothing, because a whole grand and beautiful structure will have shattered to pieces.

When you think of yourself, your world gets shrunken to you alone. While, if you think in terms of the society, your vision will remain limited up to the society. If you think in terms of nation, your thoughts will extend to the whole nation. And if your perception become global, if you have in mind, and in your thoughts, the whole world. Your vision will become a vision encompassing the unencompassable, go lapsing into rejoins beyond boundlessness... limitlessness that is infinity, as it were.

But here sir, the answer begs the question – the one who cannot develop his own self, how could he be expected to take the burden, responsibility or bear the brunt of the others' responsibility?

In fact the one who can develop himself, he alone can be thought as being a valid source of development of others. Imagine...! if every person could develop himself, this world should be a beautiful place to live in to and enjoy. And mind you, this can happen, it is possible... We can do so by doing our own part of the job – each one – doing each one's part.

But again a note of warning – developing our own self does not mean or entail or imply denying development to others or negating or ruling out others' development.

Agreed that at times it is very difficult to make others aware or conscious of their own responsibilities, but the same thing is so viable so far as we ourselves are concerned. The plus point or the bonus advantage with us is that we can do so whenever we feel like doing it and enhance our powers. – *And who does not want to be powerful these days?*

Come on, let us proceed and take our steps further and forward. Let us become responsible to ourselves, so that we may improve and develop ourselves and with that we can feel prepared to take upon ourselves the next rung in the ladder of responsibility...

Substance...

Pay attention to the following points :-

- I shall see that I take initiative to assume my responsibility myself.
- I shall take a peep into my own life to see whether I am myself getting connected with my real responsibility or not.
- The more connected do I keep myself with my responsibilities and due discharge thereof, the less complaint shall I have against life.
- The initiation of being responsible should take place from no other point but from my own self and as such, instead of making complaints against others, I shall carry out my responsibility myself with due seriousness.
- I hope I shall come out true to my own expectations and shall enhance my sense of responsibility to the requisite respectable degree.
- Being alive to and aware of my responsibility I shall duly discharge it. By doing so I shall enhance the dimensions of my success as also to take on added responsibilities.
- Together with enhancing my share of responsibilities I shall not fail to extend the dimensions of my rights too, and thereby to come out more energetic and stronger.
- While up-keeping my own stature and station, I shall continue to upbeat my own growth, so that in future I am equipped enough for being an aid to other people's successes.
- My services as an enlightened citizen will be a precious most gift to be given to the world community from my side.

Successful people do not just look for opportunities, they even create new opportunities

Opportunity not an illusion, but a reality

Whenever an unsuccessful or not so successful person is asked to tell us the reason behind his being unsuccessful, the usual answer is –'I did not get a chance to forge ahead'. Our friends also generally keep musing... Had I too got a chance, my dear, I would have been a successful man today'. Another friend who is idle and doing nothing always indulges in this kind of wishful thinking – 'How I wish, I get a good chance some day and once I do, I shall show to the world what I am - an entirely different person, incredibly outstanding – a one-in-million personality (...the kind of which did never walk on this earth... he means to add...)

The ground reality is that opportunities... chances... keep on coming and we, starting in the dark, going and standing the dark, keep on watching them and when taking advantage of those very chances, our other friends come out successful, then we regret and repent both to have let such chances pass by so easily, and end up saying – 'How I wish... I too had done the same'.

Most of our friends are not successful, not because they have no opportunities for progress, but because they do not exploit these opportunities to their advantage. They adopt a negative attitude about everything from the beginning, and develop prejudices and get stalled up where they are, passing their life in strife and in misery while others go past forging ahead.

But opportunities, in life, are dependent on what your frame of mind or your thought process is. Opportunities keep on being there, they too do wait for those people who want to take advantage of them – for, opportunities are not something abstract or illusions – they are realities – ground realities, facts of life.

Those who can shed away this illusion that 'opportunities are illusions', will start seeing the light of the day – the light of hope – in the light of which, new hopes begin to shine up.

The opportunities of success lie along with the 'hope' of success.

It is good to be optimistic... we must be optimistic. For it is this optimism that gives an inner energy that prompts us to put our steps out on the road. It is with the hope or expectation of some good coming out that our mind opens out for or admits the ideas of success and their execution.

But again, if you had expected something favourable to happen and for it did not turn out as per how you wanted, you will be disappointed – and then some other ideas – not so worthwhile – will visit you – 'oh I just wasted my time in the attempt...!' And obviously you will now not take the next step out in that direction, the direction of success or the attempt at success. And your efforts will be stalled there and in this way, despite being optimistic, you will lapse into pessimism.

Why, then, this...? The reason is that instead of being optimistic about our own selves, we tend to pin up hopes on others (for our sake).

Secondly if we have failed, we should not develop prejudices for others and should remain neutral and if we remain neutral our doors for opportunities will always remain open and not get closed for ever.

For example, supposing a clerk has not cooperated with you and your plans have been frustrated, you should not conclude from this, that all the clerks in the world are bad. If you develop this complex for the clerks, you will never try even to avail an opportunity that may revisit you in future.

In this context I may draw your attention to the following incident-

My bus, that day, had got quite late. On reaching bus stand when I got down I was surprised to see no taxi there. It was already too late in the night and my house was at a distance of about 10 kms from that place. Thoughts about home, about how to get there etc had occupied my mind while I wanted for some taxi to pass.

Suddenly my attention got drawn towards lot of commuters who were going in the direction of my locality. Thought of taking a chance with them, for a lift. I stood on one side of the road and started trying for a lift.

Several vehicles passed by and each time I waved to them, they just threw a glance at me and went past. This went on for quite some time after being ignored by about 9 or 10 such commuters. I left the idea of lift for a moment.

But the next time, suddenly, I collected my courage again and the next scooter wallah passing that side stopped. I did nothing else, I just straight away went and as if with an electric movement, I lodged myself on his scooter's rear seat.

'Where are you to go?' the fellow asked.

I put into his ears my destination. He said – 'Ok... I shall leave you' and my problem got solved.

Now, just ponder over it a little... Had I not done so, it is clear I would have lost the further chance that were coming my way.

But the point here is that it is in the hope of success roused up the zeal in me and I was able to get this new chance. I did not have to wait, nor did I have to incur any extra expenditure.

And now please note the effect of this incident. The next day when I was going towards the market, I saw a man with a bag in his hand, standing at the mill gate. A look at him showed that he too had to go further that side. I stopped the bike near him and asked where he had to go to?

He said – 'Towards Suraj Pol. My guess was right. He had to go towards Suraj Pol. I asked him to sit behind me on the bike. I took him with me up to Suraj Pol, where he got down. The smile of gratitude that he had on his face when he got down, was an enough acknowledgement for what I had done and the expression on his face is still 'imprinted' in my memory. I was over-whelmed. After this incident I made it a point to give a lift to a needy person every day, It became my practice, which continues even today...

The moral, then, is that there are many incidents, happenings around us which encourage us to understand that the 'hope' of success carries with it the 'opportunity' of success too.

When you do not have anything to lose, then why are you afraid of anything! How long will you keep waiting for the readymade opportunities! Keeping your aim in view, look for new alternatives, and proceed to grab at the new opportunities.

When I ask you to look for an alternative, I do not mean that we may plunge in without thinking that it is viable or not. Remember... looking for a new opportunity, implies 'avoiding failure' rather than losing success.

Friends, there is not and there never has been any readymade formula for success to be used and applied for getting immediate results.

Thus in each case or say every time, we have to look for a new success-formula and then go ahead accordingly. The more earnestly we look for the new opportunities, the easier our task of recognizing the opportunities becomes.

Opportunities never walk up to us, it is we who have to identify them and reach out to them.

John Johnson wanted to turn out a journal for it. About 20,000 people were made acquainted with it, urging on them to become its customers. Out of these only 3000 people only became the customers. With these people alone, the publication began and the title that was given to its was the 'The Negro Digest'.

These people were successful in this venture and after some time began publishing three magazines – Abeno, Zer and Ebony. Thus in due course, John Johnson turned out to be the owner of a very big Publication group.

We can also do the same, by recoginsing the right opportunity. Success on our part lies, in the way we take the available opportunities. If we use every opportunity for fetching success for us. Then every opportunity will turn into success.

In fact, opportunities do exists in or around us. But if we wish to take advantage of them, we have to reach out to them. They do not walk down to us. But first we have to identify them, recognise them and ensure that they are there. Then, interestingly, in this process of reaching out and identifying them, we do get wiser and capable enough and more matured to be able to even new opportunities for ourselves.

Successful people do not just look for opportunities; they even give birth to or create new opportunities.

A certain 'sick' pharmaceutical company was going to close down its establishment. At that time Deshbandhu Gupta working as a Professor at Pilani in Rajasthan, got the idea – 'why don't I buy this company myself?'

He negotiated and he bought the company for Rs. 6000/- and associating his wife Manju Gupta with it started it afresh, from a scratch.

They began handling everything – right from its packaging to distribution – themselves. They thus kept their programme of forgeing ahead and success up. The company went on growing... it is growing up even today and has taken the shape of an internationally known Company from the point of view of business – Most naturally, you would like to know its name – it's name is 'Lupin Limited'.

Now just stop to think – think it over, that if he had not created better opportunities for himself, what fate would have he met! He might have been working as worker! And as for the Company? It might have been on its last legs, counting its breaths, as it were. But he acted thoughtfully and saw a new opportunity even in its (the company's) end. He shifted his attention from the 'departing' opportunity to the 'newly arriving' one, gave his imagination a cutting edge, and deciding to give the Company the dimensions of extension, it came out successfully from the status of just a employee to a successful entrepreneur and a successful person!

Is every person able to do as he did...? Perhaps not. And that is what make some people successful and others... failures.

If considered carefully, we find that every incident or accident coming in our life, brings together with it, a promise of opportunity. It is a different matter that we are not able to see it or pin-point it. Those who are aware, they apply their discretion and turn a profound thought into a favourable situation and in this way they really come to find the seeds of a new opportunity offing in the situation. And this is... what success is all about.

Always remember – (we repeat) that successful people not only just look for new opportunities, but they can even 'create' opportunities, or say give birth to them or cause them to come into being.

It is rather curious that when an opportunity comes the way of our friends, they do not avail it, rather they ignore it and when it passes off, they run after it – what is the fun in it. What was to pass off, is gone. It is a closed chapter.

What is advantageous now is that you are once again in front of a new chance or opportunity. What is useful... now is the fact a new chance or opportunity is before us – *What is the fun now in keeping shut up...!*

Why not just grab this one that is before us and exploit it fully to our advantage and make our way forward to pave the way new and bigger opportunities...

Substance...

Pay attention to the following points :-

- I shall recognise the fact that an opportunity is a reality. It's a knock at my door, I must hear the knock.
- I shall not form any biased opinion about the opportunity, nor shall I entertain any prejudice or pre-judging. I shall keep an open mind. However first of all, I shall try to understand the reality on its merit.
- I shall always keep myself optimistic about the opportunity and it is with an optimistic and positive mind-set that I will be keeping up my work-behaviour.
- I shall keep optimistic about my own self too and in the same strain I shall keep optimistic about my success too. I shall, at the same time, go on banishing negative or pessimistic thoughts from my mind.
- I shall keep neutral vis-a-vis others, and even while being neutral, I shall keep my activeness towards the opportunities intact.
- I shall try again and again to get opportunities and shall go on trying getting them and waiting till they come.
- I shall take every advantage of the on-coming opportunities, but at the same time, I shall keep on looking out for better opportunities.
- I shall make use of every available opportunity for my success in order that I may still get more opportunities.
- I shall take my eye off the opportunities that are gone by, and shall keep concentrating on the on-coming opportunities and shall take advantage thereof to enhance the level my success.
- Any event of life, whether good or bad, has tied up to it some opportunity or the other. I shall identify and scan this opportunity carefully and then work whole-heartedly to turn it to my advantage.

Those who are successful are not angels, after all they are human beings like you and me

We are a prey to wrong concepts

Our company was having a meeting, the other day, at the Hotel Umed. In the reception hall of the hotel, a film shooting was going on at the same time. Watching a film shooting from such a close distance was my first chance that day, and I was so excited about it. We somehow, managed to find time in the Lunch break and lo! We were there at the shooting site. The actors were looking ready duly dressed up in their respective costumes as per their roles. The successful icon of film industry Amrish Puri was also there, dressed up in a king's attire.

I was dying to talk to him. I could not hold myself, and I made my way, quietly, up to him. I was hesitating to initiate talking. Unwittingly this is what I uttered –'Sir you are looking like a real king'.

He turned his head towards me and smilingly reacted –'My dear, even king's are human beings only.'

I was amazed. The smile that his sentence carried, made me so feel so light. There was nothing as I had earlier pictured in my mind. He was such a big artist and yet so simple and natural, so down to earth. He then talked to me for a while and my talking with him filled my mind, deeply, with the thought that he was just like any other person in the world.

He told me that when had come down from Jalandhar to Mumbai, he had not even a hundred rupees with him. But he got over this situation and proceeded to grow and touch new heights in the field of acting. He repeated his favorite line – 'Moghembo khush hua…'

Whenever a successful person happens to come before us, we conjure up in our mind a completely different picture of his – To us such fellows appear to be coming from an altogether different or some special background – perhaps rich and luxurious and prosperous – their dressing up, their eating habits, their ways in everything, are perceived by us as being special and stylish – they are 'higher-ups' – perhaps a little different sort – with special background, special etc etc...

And the same question is put to us, namely – 'what have you to say about yourself?' Then most of our friends would reply – 'I am not that much. I can't be that big. How can I be that high up...' etc etc. And there lies the rub. This is the attitude that makes us timid and obstructs our growth and takes away whatever there is inside us. The reason is simple, we put aside our own specialities and fall a prey to wrong complexes or beliefs or perceptions.

It is all right to keep people in high esteem but we should never forget that our success depends on what perception we have got about our own self, despite seeing and hearing things ourselves. Just as we become more aware about own-self, our thought process starts forging ahead in the right direction.

Successful people are after all human beings like you and me

Successful people do not drop from the skies, nor are they creatures from some other world. They are not strange people either. They are out of our own tribe. They are just as natural as you or I... or we all are. Facially or behaviorly they may be different. They are as human inside too, as we all are.

In fine, we should remember that successful people are after all human beings like you and me.

Nobody is high up, nor is anybody low. Nobody is higher than or lower than any other person. We are just as we all ought to or are supposed to be – that is, a human being... Our 'humanness' itself – our 'being human beings' itself – is the basis of all our successes. Thus our success would lie in the fact that in all situations we remain as natural as possible.

Now it may be (and this is life!) that people may earn money, name and fame and may make his life happy and prosperous. But in being all this or by being all this, his basic life does not change... albeit his life or living may have become better in terms of life-style and terms of quality...!

And why not? It ought to be so. We can have no grudge against it, after all it physical, facility and conveniences cannot make us comfortable, happy and prosperous, what good then is, there in being materially advanced!

Now, do you think that a man who earns more will eat food more than what he needs or his body needs! No, certainly not. In actuality, successful people are not able to make use of even a small portion of what they earn. They live not to use the things, but to make 'life' useful, meaningful, purposeful… They have a real good idea of the excellences and usefulness or purposefulness of life, and taking a cue from them, we can also attain that level or the level that we really want to attain.

Now, friends, the point is that if you do not want, no power in the world can underrate your importance. The funda is that if you yourself do not value your importance, then how could anybody else care to lift you up?

To give importance to your life and to make it more useful, the best thing is to always do what you like most. Although this can bring difficulties in your way, but you should, by no means, give up the work of your liking.

When you have to choose one pen out of the ten offered to you, obviously, you will get satisfaction out of that pen alone which you like the most.

Those persons who give up their own liking and run after other people's choices, fail to attain real success in life. Indira Nooyi, the CEO of the Pepsico company and one of the corporate world's most celebrated name, has a tell-tale incident to narrate – "I had to look for a summer job for the first time in my life when I experienced paucity of money when I was at the Yale University for my graduation. I bought a business suit for 50 dollars and reached the place of interview for that purpose. I was looking very funny in that messy sort of suit. And I was not selected. With tears in my eyes I went to my Career development counselor. He said – 'Next time in the interview you will put on a Sari which is your liking and if they cannot accept you in a Sari, the loss will be theirs and not yours'. – In my next interview by a consultant Management consultant firm, I put on a Sari and I got selected".

The moral, she said, was: 'Don't be shy of what you are. The real success lies in being content with yourself.'

Ravindra Nath Tagore tried all his life to become 'Ravindra Nath Tagore only. That is why his influence, his magic is living even today and will continue to live ever after.

You cannot get the fruit of tree while, standing under its shade. If you want the fruit, you have to make a way up to them and the moment you are able to find that way, you will get at the fruit and then enjoying its taste will become easier.

In fact the situations do not make our beliefs, instead our beliefs influence the situation or the circumstances around. If we make a right assertion or nurse right principles or beliefs, we can become competent enough to march forward on the road to progress.

You have got in you that everything...

Successful people are not influenced by circumstances, they, on the other hand it is they do themselves who influence the circumstance. But how does it happen? The fact is that they are aware that they are proceeding in the right direction. That's certainly a valuable thinking on their part. With this kind of thought process, if they continue to keep themselves connected with their basic goal. and per chance, bad days come in their life, then they do not lose their basic simplicity of thinking in the right direction.

Today if we talk about Harry Potter, his amazing success story with leave a great influence on your mind. But things were not that good with the author of this popular serial, J. K. Rolling who was leading a life of poverty after her divorce from her husband. She had become a complete loner, with her little daughter as her only company. But even then she kept herself up normal, and employed her energies in writing. As she had later revealed to a newspaper – 'In my troubled days my daughter gave me the necessary inspiration to survive.'

By the time the first novel of the series was proposed to be launched, in 1997, most of the publishers had rejected the proposal to publish it. But the same Harry Potter Series had become so popular that people had begun to line up early in the morning in the front of the vegetable seller and to obtain a copy of the publication. Now was another day and Rolling was happy and prosperous both.

The feeling about your own self that... – 'I am prone to succeed in my career to the same extent as other friends of mine are in their fields' – generates a valuable feeling in you which says that you have got that everything in you that is needed to be there in any person who wants to be successful. This feeling whenever experienced generates in us a valuable thought that implies that success does not lie in circumstances; but in our beliefs.

In fact, nobody is big or small – it is a person's thinking that is big or small. No individual is any special person, what is special is his thought. With our special thoughts, the situations automatically tend to become 'special'.

By pushing up your level of thinking, you can push up your status

Bobby Jindal, only 24, became the Health Minister of the American province of Louisiana. By his resourcefulness, he was able to bring about positive and practical changes to policies relating to public health and thus he was able to carve out a special place for himself in the matters relating to national policies. Therefore he stood as a candidate for governorship of Louisiana state but he lost the election by a small margin. But he again fought the next elections time and came out victorious by a huge margin.

At the time of joining the post of the Governor, Bobby Jindal was easily the youngest of all Governors, the special point being that he had no political background. It was about 50 years back that his father Shri Amar Chand Jindal from Khanpura village (India) had gone to America and had settled there. By dint of his right thinking and correct manner of doing things, he was able to reach such enviable position of success.

If one has got will to make progress, one can pave his way to highest level, because, I repeat – success does not lie in the circumstances, but in turning circumstances into success.

Those people, who step out of the bondage or bounds of circumstances, are often able to turn them to their advantage. In doing such things, they do not see or bother about other people's opinions or what other may be thinking about their actions, on the other hand they are all the time thinking about how the quality of life can be improved. What really happens is that by putting their abilities to proper use, they make quality of their life better... This is what success is – By lighting up uour level of thinking we can always enhance our status in life.

It is really a good thing... that status is not something that is available in the market, to be brought home in a carry bag at our sweet will. It is something that is promoted and prompted from within. That's why we should keep the level of our thinking high up and raise our life-style or the quality of life higher up. In fine, the time is, or say the call of the times — is that — *we must come out of the narrow shells of thinking into bright.*

Then, come, let us change our way of thinking and let's feel that we are perfectly all right so far as our present situation or abilities are concerned. We have certain specialties in ourselves that are definitely paying and rewarding enough in the long run. Let us, with this 'equipment', go ahead to forge our way to prosperity and happiness...

Substance...

Pay attention to the following points :-

- I am a human being too like others and there is no difference whatsoever between me and them.
- I shall entertain good thoughts about others and wish that the same be done for my own thoughts.
- Successful people are by no means different or peculiar. They too are just like other common people. This means that I can be successful too following my own different way, just as others have been following their own peculiar ways.
- I shall try to remain my natural self in all circumstances; I shall always remain what I am.
- I shall admire those persons whose life-style and quality of life are commendable. I shall try to take my life forward too in that direction.
- I shall try to understand what is excellent in my life and shall push up my life forward in that direction.
- I shall do things that I really like and thereby shall enhance the value and the importance of my life and my identity.
- I shall never feel shy of my situation and shall make due progress on the strength of my own worth and shall thus prove my usefulness.
- I shall not be influenced by the conditions around, but instead shall influence the situations by employing my own mode of thinking.
- I shall keep my energies directed towards my principal goal, unmindful of the difficulties and obstacles coming in the way.
- I shall keep on enhancing the level of my thinking as also that of my station in life.

Success not at the mercy of 'means'

Means do not work on their own, they are governed by us

The other day I went to the Bank with a relative of mine who had to get his money fixed deposited. He told me that one Mr. Vishnu Prasad of the Bank was known to him and the fellow would get his work quickly done.

We straight away went to Vishnu Prasadji. I saw him closely and found that he was physically handicapped. He was lean and thin and he looked so weak. But there was a wonderful glow of energy on his face. He gave us all the help.

I observed that every now and then his colleagues had been consulting him in one way or the other. He was readily giving all the necessary information and at the same time was giving them necessary tips also.

Our work over, we found that he was guiding the man in-charge of updating the data in computer and explaining how to do it in a correct and nice manner.

We came out but not without musing over the facts that Vishnu Prasadji was a handicapped person, completely disadvantaged, his staff-fellows were all fit and fine and active. But despite this, they all seemed so dependent upon Vishnu Prasadji who, by now, you may have come to gather, was expert in his work.

Who would you consider successful to? –Vishnu Prasad or his colleagues? – Obvious answer is Vishnu Prasadji.

I felt, after being a few minutes in his presence, that he was person who generated energy into others. I too felt myself so energetic after having passed a few minutes in his company at the Bank. The irresistible conclusion was that the basic energy in him had made such a positive impact on his ability and efficiency in his work. In fact, his efficiency and capacity never stopped getting enhanced.

After we look around and find successes around us, we start thinking that the secret of those successes are the costly resources. But this is not true. The costly resources are not successes, they are only conveniences. Had this not been true the people with resource alone would have made greater progress, and the poor people would have become still far weaker.

The progress that we find all around is not so much due to resource, but because of the proper use of these resources. The important point here is that no resources can operate without our will, the reason being that the means do not operate on their own, they are caused to be operated by us.

Even the best of TVs do not get started until we switch the remote on. Even thereafter it shows us those channels only that we wish to watch. Without the intervention of man, every means is useless.

Why even after all the computerization in the Banks, the Bank people still do a part of their clerical work manually — so that if the computer data saved is washed off the manually kept accounts record still remains with them and all is not lost for ever. Another example is the intervention of the class room teacher despite all the audio visual aids including computers.

These examples show that whatever success is attained is not mainly due to the resources employed, but is really due to the balance between a man's of heart and mind. A person, who succeeds in living the life with this poise, becomes a man with resources and the rest are poor and helpless.

Come... let us talk it over a little more candidly. It is commonly believed that we are able to see because of the eyes. But this is not true or the truth. If we had been able to see because of the eyes, then we would have been able to see everything clearly even in the dark. But fact is not so. When we are in the darkness we will see only darkness even when eyes are open.

The truth is that we apprehend and perceive things and events with our heart. The information about the feeling that the heart experienced is transmitted straight to the mind. In this way the transmission of information between the heart and the mind goes on taking place. But the heart, at this, does not take any decision of its own. The decision-taking always rests with the mind. The eyes when got connected with the mind, are able to see things only as they are and it, thus, becomes the witness to the event.

When we work keeping the correct balance between the two, heart and mind, then all our resources, physical or material, become our means of success.

Success is not necessarily slave of the best means

We have already discussed above that the atmosphere of success does not get created because of the means. The means get developed due to the atmosphere of success that is created. If is these means resulting from this favourable atmosphere play a helping role in the execution of the work. But despite all this the person which entails the support of means of success is none else but we ourselves. That's why success depends not on the means, but on our own self.

In a class of students up to 50 in number only one gets the first rank. It's not the quality of pencil, rubber or some such other thing that is responsible for his first rank. It is the quality of answers written at the dictates of his mind that is responsible for his first rank.

Similarly, a sportsman becomes the fastest athlete of the world not just because of the quality of his shoes, or the quality of the track. It's the quality of the ability of his feet that makes him the fastest runner.

Remember therefore, that success is never at the mercy of the quality of the 'means'.

The truth is perhaps the other way round. It is the means that are at the mercy of success. Means are meaningless if they do not entail success.

This is not to say that good and quality equipment has no meaning in life. If you are performing well and to add to it, you are given quality and highly developed means, your quality or efficiency will definitely show an enhancement in its degree.

As happens with an important letter written in hand as against one typed out with a type-writer or a computer print thereof, but what if the person in question does not know how to write at all, computer will be a meaningless thing for him!

It is the performance that justifies the quality of the means used in the performance. Success banks principally on the skill rather than on the equipment used.

It is you yourself who add value to lend perfection to the means...

A person who is aware of his means, will always be more aware of or conscious of the use of the means, like a good driver who will always be conscious of the need of timely oiling of the engine and other things like it. This consciousness of the better use of equipment connects the person with the ultimate aim behind the activity. Thus he is able to perform better, the reason being that his attention is not so much towards the deficiency in the means as towards the means themselves that he has and towards their better use.

Sushmita Sen revealed, the other day, in a TV interview that the gloves she had put on her hands on the first round of Miss Universe competition, were made from the ordinary gloves worn in the feet, and were got prepared by her tailor. Despite this she won the crown of Miss Universe. Her hand gloves did not prove any minus point, rather their glory – the glory of the gloves – was enhanced. The moral is that the equipment used in a successful performance are a credit to the equipment too.

Adorned with innumerable international honours, the India Scientist Madhava Nayyar the Chairman of ISRO contributed richly to the making of the first multi-dimensional satellite projectile device SLV-3 and PSLV. What is remarkable is that it was first time in the last two decades that a non-specialist satellite scientist was given this honoured post. And add to this the fact he was a scientist who did not hold a doctorate degree.

A few words about his background – he was born a small village of the Kanyakumari district, got his primary education while residing in a hutment in a village know as Tirunandkara. While he was just in class X, he, along with his friends had manufactured a radio-driven aeroplane with the help of the airways wreckage waste material. This activity was not there in his syllabus.

In this way, with the help of very elementary means, his steps took him to the field of space science and he made great strides as a scientist in that field.

When a man is conscious of and keen about the equipment he is using, every aspect of his performance begets an automatic quality. In fact, all the parts of the means of the success, work in unison and in full swing and with perfection and wholesomeness.

The important point I wish to make is that it is not the means themselves but it is you who give these means or the equipment a completeness. And that is exactly why we rightly say that success lies not in the means but in making the means successful by rendering them useful.

As we advance on the path of progress, doors of the success in future go on opening automatically.

The real strength lies in our mind

Those people, who tend to think beyond their adversities, can and do pay more attention to making their means more suitable and valuable. Thereby they are able to put their physical and bodily instruments to their optimum use.

The world fame astrophysicist and professor of Maths Dr. Stephen Hawking had developed a disease known as 'ALS'. You may have seen and heard this great man on the TV screen quite often. He does all his daily chores sitting on a wheel-chair. Due to his ailment he can neither speak properly nor move his hand or legs. Not only this, except for his body and mind, all other parts or organs are quite useless. That's why most of his tasks are rendered with great difficultly.

Despite so many weakness and handicaps, Prof Hawking made that great discovery – the discovery of 'black hole' – as the originating point of the evolution of the universe and by this discovery of his, he succeeded in unfolding the mystery of the universe.

Later on April 2007 he executed the wonderful feat of flying in the space with weightlessness and zero gravitation, sitting in a private jet aeroplane. On this achievement of his he stated – 'I wish to show that any of us can experience this state of weightlessness.'

The lesson we learn from Prof. Hawking's life is that the real strength lies not in the means or resources, but in our own mind. If the mind is strong, the resources can be made stronger. Thus our life can be made stronger. It can be made stronger by relieving ourselves from the worry of the want of means or resources.

Those person who are able to reconcile with things which are not favourable to them, with the help of the ways suggested above, can easily turn the circumstances into their favour. In fact what happens is that in a given state of situation they are able to identify the means which help them in proceeding ahead.

Om Prakash Gurjar, who is a social activist has been working for the cause of child labour and bonded labour, since the early days of his career. He was awarded the prestigious International Peace for children Award 2007. He had challenges before him even from the very childhood. He was born in a very humble hutment in a very remote village of Saradhana Dhani, some 2 kilometers away from the village Dwarapur.

When he was just 5 years old, his parents pushed him into bonded labour. He was subjected to hard labour for the next three years. He was turned out from there when he was just eight years old. A 'social home' adopted him thereafter.

During the time he stayed at Ashram, he, secretly began to help the remaining children working as bonded labour in that particular village and other villages also. He initiated the programme 'Village-Children's Friends'. The programme had such an impact that now the children's birth-rights are not violated, children are not engaged in or pushed into bonded labour.

This is a very good example of fighting a meaningful battle with limited resources against the darkness of poverty, despondency, and helplessness. Obviously this success had resulted not due to the realisation of his weakness, but on account of the realisation and understanding of his strength and of how it can be put to use.

Such examples teach us that in this world, the helpless are not those who do not have means or resources, but are those who 'are pretending to feel handicapped' for want of means or resources. The success really lies not in any other thing than 'in' the person who gets to develop means or resources for success.

There are some sensitive souls amongst our friends too, and it sometimes happens that realisation of developing such resources which may help us to fight against evils prevailing in the life around and thereby removing these evils and thus make life more comfortable and worth-living. Inspired by such genuine sentiment and then by developing appropriate means of making our life a quality life and a life worth-living. – Therein lies our success... What else is success than this?

Graham Bell fell in love with a deaf girl while he was teaching her how to teach language to the deaf. He wanted to make a machine whereby her deaf friend would be able to hear. The idea of making a telephone struck him and he pulled himself up to the job with all the determination and devotion at his command. He thought that just as the small layer at the screen of the ear can vibrate the tiny bones of the ear, in the same way a metal (iron) layer could vibrate an iron structure too. Thus, he thought, that the transmission of spoken words through the medium of a telephone might be viable too. Graham Bell and his team kept stuck to this mission and ultimately they were able to invent the instrument Telephone.

Friends..., Love is a power that can make a weak mind also strong. It can remove weakness in an object and can give birth to a new kind of power. Love is the fountain source of all powers in our life. The phenomenon called 'Love' does not originate from any other outside agency, it is born within ourselves. Steeped in love we can attain all those powers that we want to acquire. But at the same time we should be clear in our mind that one who loves his own self alone, can love others.

Such of our friends who make the mistake of treating their means or resources as their masters, always feel stressful and disgusted. Why so...? The reason is that they have an inner fear of being deprived of them – the means, which they wrongly treat as being their masters.

We should never forget this basic thing, namely, the means do not bring about human development, it is the man who develops means does so. As such, we should develop means on the strength of our fundamental trait humanity. Considerations of humanity should be our flagship, and now having known this, *we should ever be prepared place humanity and human consideration at our disposal to us. When the need arises.*

Come on, let's now reiterate the need of making our resources more powerful, so that by making them more useful we can exploit them to their maximum for our benefit and further by reinforcing these means successfully, we can with the help of these facilities and conveniences make our life, day-to-day life, more comfortable and enriching...

Substance...

Pay attention to the following points :-

- I shall try to be physically and mentally effecient and shall use this efficiency as a means of my achievements.
- Using the resources as a means of my achievements, I shall not let my efficiency to be played down.
- I shall conduct my resources rightly and thereby keep on constantly adding to my efficiency.
- I shall keep up the necessary balance between my heart and mind, and shall keep on becoming still more resourceful and prosperous.
- At my work place, I shall create the necessary atmosphere in keeping with my equipment/facilities and shall constantly keep on making necessary improvements therein.
- I shall devote my attention to make better use of the resources currently available with me, rather than to harp on the want thereof. By doing so I shall arrive at a situation in which I could obtain better resources.
- My real power lies in my mind. Being aware of this fact, I shall make my mind stronger and shall thereby make my resources more powerful.
- I shall turn my biggest weakness into my strength, and counting on it I shall make my life and all others people's life more comfortable and convenient.
- I shall highlight and exploit my strengths in a modest, courteous and loving manner and shall seek and discover newer means of development.

No work is special, the way of doing it is special

We get used to get into a rut

Most of our friends make use of the same ways in their work which have been followed through for years. They just tread on the same old ways, the beaten track, and are not able to bring about any marked changed in the work. They are doing that much of work as they are used to be doing, they become the slaves of their own customary mode of working. They even live in their own shells and do not try to come out of them. They tolerate their own failure. Sometimes they are prone to nurse a mixed feeling of regret, prejudice and the smallness and insignificance of their work. They think that their own work has not won any mileage for them and they begin finding other people's jobs more significant.

This, it is submitted, is not a correct approach. Had there no work been done, how could so much of progress in the world be made. We would have stayed there itself, where we were thousands of years back. The reality is different. In fact the fault does not lie in the work under discussion, the fault lies with us-that is, and with those who are supposed to do the particular work.

No work becomes successful on its own; it gets success by its having been done it properly.

Habits die hard, and once we create a particular style for doing a work, it becomes our habit. And the established habit does not easily make room for new ideas for doing that work, and the old habit is not given up easily, with the result that we go on putting up with the tradition that has got developed.

In fact, what we need is self introspection, self analysis, analysis of the manner in which we are doing the work. This analysis can become our eye-opener. We can analyse the utility of the manner in which we are doing a certain work. And finally we are able to get at the new and better manner which can make us accomplish our task more successfully and easily.

New ways, serve to add the element of novelty to the work

The best way to adopt new ideas about the manner of doing a work is to give up the old methods and ways and let them get out from our mind. The old idea will make room for the new ideas. But this involves serious thought being given to the new ideas and then to adopt such new ideas as are able to procure for the work a new identity. The profounder the manner of work, the more presentable it will become. In this way we would be able to present our work with added success (Just as good presentation of delicious dishes adds value to the food).

Dainik Bhasker of Rajasthan was launched on 19th December 1996 from Jaipur. Its publication had new features – a larger number of pages, Colour-print in place of black and white pictures, new columns and information, and an attempt to present the smallest material in a newer manner. This initiative of Bhaskar not only carved a proper place in the hearts of the readers but it also prompted or, say compelled other papers also to adopt new methods. The publication Bhaskar thus was able to go ahead and create a new segment of readers and this had its impact on other parts of the country too.

Before initiating the Paper, the Bhaskar group conducted a survey on a big scale and tried to know what material the public expected from the Paper. This feedback proved important. The satisfaction of readers became the secret of the popularity of the newspaper. On 20th Dec 2012, the paper completed its existence of 10 years and at this point again this group (Bhaskar Group) put up a new objective to be achieved in the course of its journey of growth namely – 'to make this Paper the 'world's biggest paper and the Group to be the biggest media house' in the world'.

Giving up old ideas does not at all mean giving up every idea. It only means not to be too active on the points which are likely to add to our failure. We however should not give up those precious ideas which are likely to prove useful in our work. Just as, along with the rubbish of the house and office, we do not throw away valuable things like jewellery, cash, mobile etc.

That explains why we do not bring the rubbish back while we keep valuable articles at home or in office very carefully and safe.

The same principle applies to our ideas also. If we do not throw out of our mind useless ideas, they will spoil our minds and if we do not preserve and collect useful ideas, they will be put into oblivion and will be lost so far as we are concerned. Therefore wisdom lies in the fact that we should go on forgetting useless ideas and keep useful ideas safe deposited in the mind.

At the end of this process we will find that our mind is abundantly filled with good and useful ideas. At the same time, we will be able to find ways and means of our reaching out to those new techniques which are useful for us. This shows that the new technique add a sense of novelty to the work.

Those who make a correct estimation of there strengths before starting a work, they are bound to develop a correct attitude towards it.

Not the work, but our attitude is big or small

No work is either big or small. It is in fact, our attitude towards it that is big or small. It depends on how we look at it. If the work which is in our head is considered by us to be big. It's final outcome will definitely be found far more improved and useful satisfying and even great.

Madam E. J. Walker's financial situation was not good. During these hard times Walker started working on an idea relating to the increased growth of hair and hair dressing in respect of the African women. She got success in the project and she was encouraged to take more work. She employed the successful trick in her further work. Later on, this technique came to be known as Walker process. This resulted in removal of her poverty and she went on progressing with success. You will be glad to know that she was first Afro-American woman to become a multimillionaire.

Those who dare to cross the limitations imposed by customs, culture and civilization, and transcending these limits do something successful, they serve to present themselves as an example or a model, and those who observe them, also are subjected to cause changes in these ideas – those who could never dare touch a big or small task for the fear of something going wrong.

Kiran bedi was the first woman to become an IPS officer. She chose a province or field of life which was always dominated by males for a long time. Women hesitated to come to this side for their career purposes. But by taking a meaningful leap forward she opened up a new avenue of opportunities for the coming generation. Not only this but by sheer dint of her merit and talent, she was able to win for the police the world over a new identity.

This kind of success does not get caused by just a police uniform. One gets it by adopting newer ways of getting success. The same old kind of work, but by her successful new methods and ways, she made the work unique.

This goes to prove that speciality or uniqueness does not lie in the work, but in the person who does that work.

As has Kiran Bedi said – "For me it was never a means to get power. When in uniform, I was there only as a citizen. To stop crime was always my first priority."

The attitude that we have towards our work is responsible for the kind or measure of success we, in the end, get. As such our success or failure does not depend on our work only but on the attitude with which we involve ourselves in it. This goes to show clearly that, it is our attitude and not the work that is big or small.

By adopting a special attitude towards work, we may evolve special ways or methods of executing it too.

No work is special, only the way in which it is does... is special

'We should always try for excellence as well as perfection. It is immaterial whether the work is trivial or small or petty. 'Excellence' and perfection – no other option is to be made acceptable.'

J. R. D. Tata, The Founder Chairman of the Tata Group

If you wish to achieve something substantial in life, do not think – 'whether I should do it?' let your ideas drift towards this instead – Why can't this be done? I must do it. Giving this suggestion to yourself is important – 'Why can't this work be done?' the moment you entertain this idea in your mind, you are directly 'in' the job that is you have already started trying to find out the ways of doing it. This prompts you to take improve upon the ways and means of doing the job, That, again, makes you and your identity special.

A certain manufacturing company making consumer products launched its new product some time back. The Company claimed that the taste of the product was good. In order to establish this claim and to make it stronger and more effective the Company Executive so managed that the different customers made it a point to taste it. People began to accept this special way and the result was that the sale of its product went on increasing. The company thus adopting this new method had acted with imagination, and imagination is a very important element in matters of production and sale both.

Friends, thus we may conclude here that success lies in your special talent, rather, than in the work. That's why again, success lies not in just doing the work, but in doing it in a special manner. This special manner make the work special.

Always remember – No work is special, only the way in which it is does... is special.

The question that arises here is – 'How to get at these special ways' or – 'to develop better ways' – 'how to make even the smallest process or act excellent.'

The answer to all these questions, again, is – 'Imagination'. Add the element of 'imagination' to your task and it will result in success. The very thought of success breeds in your mind the 'success'.

Thus the man with imagination is prone to achieving success. Naturally he kind of comes to 'inaugurate' his better ways. Imagination adds a new 'strangeness' of things and this 'strangeness' adds to the beauty of the act and makes it more exciting for him and interesting and attractive for others. Again, the moral is – imagination adds 'to the excellence' and excellence adds to 'a feel-good' element to the work and the end result is... 'success'.

The great scientist Albert Einstein used to say – Being imaginative is more important than being 'knowledgeable'. To first know the task a little, and then to 'add' imagination' to it. The result would be 'a newer thing, or newer process' and what else is success but a feeling good factor vis-à-vis newer skill.

The very nature or the very native function of 'imagination' is to give 'new angles' of looking at the things, and 'the new thoughts' add the element of speciality to it. And with this we are able to accomplish something different and special.

Here doing 'newer' things does not mean doing 'some new unsuccessful' thing again. That could never be our aim.

If you wish to make Rajasthani Mirchi Bada, you have to adopt and follow the due procedure. You are supposed to first heat up the oil in the frying pan and then fry the 'besan-wrapped' spice mixture. But if you do not heat up the oil and instead drop the mixture in the 'cold' oil, you will and not end up with making Mirchee Badas, it would be an unsuccessful dish. The moral, therefore, is new methods but not at the cost of losing sight of your goal.

Examples of 'novelty' or imaginativeness of manner can be multiplied.

In a small village lived a young man who ran a provision shop. Several people of the village were residing at other places where they had gone for work and to earn money. The village people had to talk to these men, their relatives, quite often. This fellow started an STD booth just adjacent to his shop. By and by people started flocking in at the booth. Everyday a large number of villagers came to use the booth. The young man observed this seriously and started to think what more he could do to attract the people to the booth and to see that they got the facility of talking freely to their relatives outside.

Here a new idea struck him. And what he did was that he bought mobiles (cell-phones) of 5 different companies and with the mind that through them people could do outgoing calls at the minimum rate or almost free.

Now, whenever somebody came to him in order to talk to his relatives, he would supply him the cell phone of the Company whose number the relative brought with him. Then he would arrange that the persons talked on mobile phone of that particular company at a cheap rate. This facility proved useful and cheap for the people and they started coming in still larger numbers. By this new arrangement there was a quick boost-up in the young man's earnings. The customers also could talk at a lesser cost.

Now see that it was just a very ordinary step. In the ordinary course, he would have pulled on with this basic STD booth, but since he had a creative idea in mind he did not stop as he thought that better way of work would always give good results.

Naturally better way here meant a new and creative strategy. The result was that he was able to give cheaper and better services to his customers and in the process, he also learned that, the success envisaged included and implied better and cheaper service to the consumers. It may be noted that in the course of such processes, the person himself grows too, and prepares himself for making and meeting the next change.

Whenever there is a talk about some work or task, we are often told that we should do the work in such and such particular way, or that it is not good to do like this or do like that. But inspite of all this, the person who really reaches the highest point of success is the one who evolves his own ways and manners of doing the work. It is obvious that when he would do a particular work, thinking that it is good for him or that he is comfortable at it, developing new techniques become easier for him. He realises that *particular time is meant for making this work more valuable.*

Come on then, let's do certain tasks which have not been done so far, let us tread those paths of success which people are dying to tread or walk on. The idea is that, when we become successful, we may tell others that this can happen, and further, by saying so, we can encourage them to do things warranting something different and something new to be done, and thereby unfolding the mystery of our story of success...

Substance...

Pay attention to the following points :-

- I shall proceed with the assumption that no work is a success by itself. I shall therefore cause it to be a success in my own way, by my own acumen.
- I shall pay due attention to the manner of doing my work, and for doing it in a still better way, I shall bring about changes in the traditional mode of work.
- Including new and novel concepts in my work, I shall give my work a new look, a new identity and then present it successfully before others.
- People's satisfaction – that will be my main concern and aim every time and on all occasions.
- I shall conserve and keep safe all my new and precious ideas and thoughts concerning my work, doing away with all redundant ideas. With the result that I will be having with me a rich treasure of precious ideas and thoughts.
- I shall consider the work that is with me to be most useful and important and shall be making it the basis of my success. At the same time I shall respect the work of others too.
- By taking bold and meaningful initiatives I shall present myself as an example before others and by doing so I shall pave the way for them and serve them by being a guide.
- I shall connect my work with imagination, and adopting the resultant special modes of work, I shall use them for making my work all the more special.
- I shall keep myself connected with the mindset of doing always 'better than before' and shall proceed in the direction of making it excellent in every way.

The World does not 'make' stars, it is on a look out for them

To do exactly as other do, is a sick-mentality

One evening I was enjoying listening to a music programme telecast on Television Young singers were giving their performances, one by one. The atmosphere around was charged with the chill of competitive spirit. It was a very enriching experience, as the judges sitting in the front were making expert comments with their analytical and scanning remarks.

In the chain of the items, certain young performer presented a song-number. The judge got damned serious as they listened to him. The entire atmosphere suddenly became grave. The audience assumed a pin-drop silence posture. The Judge was looking at the young performer as the performer looked at the Judge.

After a brief spell of silence, the Judge broke the ice and said, addressing the singer – 'young man there is no music in you down there. So whatever energy you have in yourself, use it at the correct place. Study hard, know your capabilities and put in your knowledge and energies in the right direction". Saying all this, be placed the truth in front of all.

The reaction that instantaneously took place in the mind of the young fellow indicated that he had understood what the former had said.

It is often the case that whenever we see others doing something, say like singing – we feel for a while that the utmost happiness in the world lies in singing. We have a similar feeling or reaction when we see somebody dancing or dance. We sort-of begin feeling that our entire salvation lies in singing or dancing only. We are so inspired that we feel like leaving everything else and take to or adopt such kinds of things and get the unknown and utmost pleasure.

In a bid to get this unknown pleasure, we tend to forget our own life. The psyche behind all this is that when we see the so-called celebrities, we start nursing a wish to adopt their life-style and making ourselves believe that, that style should be our ultimate in life. When we see a film, its hero becomes our fond dream, our ideal, and similarly when we see a cricketer hitting shots all around and getting big applause from the crowd – we begin being crazy after him. and he becomes our 'fantasy'. When we see a wealthy man, we secretly begin admiring him desiring him to be our ideal.

Thus when we begin running after other people's successes and do not get anything any result out of it, we get disappointed and in that frustration we begin to have an inferiority complex or a guilt-feeling about our own self. And in these moments of frustration life becomes vain for us and not worth living.

The question – the big question is – Can somebody else's success render our success useless? Can our life become worthless, if we do not get the kind of success others get? The answer is: ... Never.

The problem (and the reality) is that on seeing others' success we tend to forget our own identity. And then what follows is that instead of trying for things on the strength of our own identity, we come to take recourse to attempts or tactics which push us off towards failures instead of successes. Thus we ourselves become the cause of our own failures.

The truth is that to do exactly as other do, or to imitate others blindly is no wisdom; This is sick-mentality. Although we several times tend to do as others do, to imitate or copy others knowingly or unknowingly, but we must remember that a sick attempt can never give healthy results. The reason is that no two persons can be exactly similar to each other, their faculties being different. The person 'A' will make progress in his field, while 'B' will do so in his field, depending on how much control they have in their respective fields.

Yes, of course, we can learn a lot from the other people's failures or successes provided, we remain conscious and aware of our own identity, our own existence, our own strengths and capabilities.

If we do not adopt this principle there is every chance of our going astray from our path. Who can help a person who is too eager and willing to stray off from the right path?

Life and our existence carries so much relevance and meaning...

A person comes to this world with limitless faculties at his command. In this world man is the only creature who has got the great powers of going beyond the highest point in the space and the deepest places in the ocean, and can cross most difficult of obstacles and challenges coming in the way. We should also remember that human life is the most excellent of Nature's creations and that we do not get it again and again. Therefore, it will be wise for us to make the best of it before its slips off our hands.

But, the unfortunate part is, most of us tend to seek our faculties in the characters of other people. The result is that we belong to nowhere. We keep on seeking our qualities in others, which is a useless exercise and do not take us anywhere. We lose our way and by the time we realize our mistake, life is found to be left much behind.

What is its reason? The reason in one word is 'Comparison'. We begin to compare our life with others' lives, not giving due weight to the relevance of our own life. We become a victim of this tendency of comparing our own selves with others and in this process, we fall a prey to the ungratifiable greed and desires and ambitions all our life, which is nothing but only running after illusions, a purposeless pursuit, an irrelevant exercise.

In most of the cases it is found that the moment we look to somebody else's progress, we try to kind of install a weighing balance with its two pans before our eyes, placing ourselves in one pan and in placing the other person in another pan and thus seek to compare ourselves with that other achiever. Our whole attention gets focused to that other person's progress. The result is obvious. Instead of looking after and taking care of our own progress, we waste our time in looking at other people's progress.

We get lost in this process of 'Comparison' and in the process we lose our pace of progress because our attention for doing our own things better, shifts to other people's work. All this results in hampering our efficiency and progress, and we become passive towards our goal and become rather inert. We get concerned about others progress rather than worrying about our own.

Most of our friends are unsuccessful not because, they cannot do anything, but because others are able to do something. RajuRam is happy with his own house until the time Gangaram lives in a rented house. But the moment

Gangaram gets a grand house made for him, Rajuram's happiness melts off and turns into sorrow. –Why? –Because, his own house doesn't appear to be a house anymore and seems to him to be like a simple hut now. This gives rise in him to a feeling of inferiority. The reason again is that he has taken to that unwarranted practice called 'comparison'.

We want ourselves to progress, but we wish at the same time that others should not progress. This is pure and simple jealousy, although it doesn't lie in our power or our wish to hold somebody's progress.

We should realize that, it is no use having wishes or desires that do not let us make progress or that come in our way of making progress!

It has been often seen, that in this all mad race of comparison and of our unwarranted concern with other people that we lose our way and go too far away out of the track into the 'tunnels of darkness of confusion. We begin to lose and see hope our dreams are shattered and we come to experience a sense of disillusionment. The charm of life is lost and we feel frustrated, and in a situation like this even thoughts of suicide come in our mind. In the very presence of life itself, life becomes lifeless; The objective is lost, but there is nobody else responsible for this paradox except we our own selves. There is no outside agency responsible for this. It is we who are guilty of whole lapse because we made the basic mistake of assessing ourselves through the wrong medium or means namely 'Comparison'.

In fact, life and our existence carries so much relevance and meaning. It is, however we ourselves who are bent on making it irrelevant, and meaningless.

In the process of evaluation with other's success, one always is in a losing mode

It sounds very strange when some golf player says, "I want to become a player like Tiger Woods". By saying this, he unwittingly and unknowingly puts a limit on all the possibilities of his own game. Therefore, his goal now gets limited to become something not beyond Tiger Woods game. It is a state of mind where he stops using his own faculties of mind, but relies on other people's wisdom. The cause, again, is 'comparison', and there are attempt at imitation. He makes the assessment of his faculties in terms of other people's success. In this process of evaluation, he always is in a losing mode. And in such a situation, he cannot go too far on the road to success.

It is good to have an ideal, but to make that ideal your own limit, is not at all a correct approach. It is wrong thinking. A wise and thoughtful player would think like this, "I want to become a successful golfer". With this thought he is able to find and acquire those fine things about the game which would inspire him beyond a point of limit and take him far ahead on the road to efficiency.

Again we can behave and do like this provided we do not resort to that monstrous thing 'Comparison'.

Our success doesn't depend on any other basis, but depends on the basis on which we make our own assessment. The reason is that every incident of our life taking place is influenced by our own assessment or evaluation.

A correct assessment and analysis of our own capabilities and potential definitely enhances the chances of our success

A thing does not outlive its utility or does not become useless until we believe it to be useless, the reason being that changes do occur in it, but its basic features or qualities or elements still persist in it. Knowing this, those persons who look at things on the basis of their basic features are able to asses and analyse correctly their capabilities or potential.

Tsoi Shiro Honda, the founder of world-famous Honda Motors company looking at an out of use and junk-like engine got an idea to the effect that the said engine could be fitted in on a bicycle so that it might run as a car. He worked on this idea and was able to make, what is these days, called a motor cycle. Today the Honda Motor-cycle is the heart-throb of lacs of motorcyclists of the world.

Such great successes make us aware of the principle that those who make a correct assessment and analysis of their capabilities, are able at the same time, to blossom them and enhance them a great deal and then by using them in their work, are able to attain new heights in the field of their work. But those who do not do all this, they remain passive with their capabilities though by their not wanting to work the capabilities are not thereby put to an end.

The important point is – how can the qualities in-built in us can be developed? – The answer is by 'self-enrichment'. By self enrichment we mean that we may go on imbibing in ourselves those inherent qualities of ours that are essential for success, and we may go on giving up those evils which serve to create obstacles in the way of success. By repeatedly and continuously doing so we may be able to develop in ourselves, good qualities or virtues.

The more a person enriches himself with qualities or virtues, the more eager and particular he becomes in highlighting his own star and making it shine more brightly.

The world does not make stars... it is on a look out for them.

Whenever I meet somebody, the fellow tries, indirectly during conversation, to find out or actually asks – 'Around how much do you earn? Or 'what do you get from this work in terms of money?' This means that 'the other person' is interested more in the things I have, than in me.

He perhaps does not know that had I no existence of my own, who would have brought those outward things that he notices around me. They are there 'because of the fact that they mean to be important for me.

But no sir, mindset is mindset and these a typical 'materialistic' trait in people – a weakness in people to see everything and everybody not in terms of humanity but in terms of money, weighing not the virtues in him, but what, in terms of money, he can fetch. In other words, people have the tendency today to think that only money or wealth is the measure of all that goes by the name 'success' or life.

They don't realise that yes, money and wealth do help us in the achievement of our success. But no, success cannot be achieved by money alone. Success and money cannot be, need not be and should not be equated. It is mean, petty, inhuman and vulgar way of looking at people and things. I would call it even cynical. Moreover success will money is not the real success. Real success is much ahead of these material norms – Yes, far-far ahead.

As against all this, those who are not prey to this weakness, never sell gold at the rate of iron. For them what is important is success and they do not want to lose it. Instead they employ their success in polishing and in shining up their own basic qualities, virtues, characteristics, capabilities and potential, and their work and they themselves thus rise up and shine all over with their own gloss, own brilliance – and then, the world calls them 'stars' – stars in the sky of the society.

But then all this can only happen when we do not waste our time in irrelevant pursuits and give our specialties the right kind of treatment – the right kind here would mean 'that is in tune with our basic nature or temper'. With this approach we can in future, attain the kind of stardom we, in fact, want.

Take an interesting example – supposing a man is going to the office in his car worth crores of rupees and suddenly something wrong goes with the car and car suddenly refuses to get started. The man comes out and tries, but no, the car does not get started…, Naturally seeing no way out, the owner of car calls a mechanic. The mechanic with a playful smile on his face and humming the tune of some song and with a very casual air goes to the car and does something and within 5 minutes the engine gets to throb again indicating that car is back in order. Now, let us stop here for a moment to think as to who the 'star' in this situation is. The apparent answer is 'mechanic bhai'!

Thus like the mechanic in our story, one can be a star – by sheer dint of his qualities – and we often see that the world, stupefied as it were, with this brilliance, runs after him in sheer fascination.

Always remember – the world does not make the stars. It is on a look up for them. In fact, the star is the person himself, and once he becomes a star, the rest of things automatically follow and come to him as a necessary corollary. He don't have to make special effort for them.

No work runs because it results in gain, it runs because it has some 'utility' (usefulness) in it. Thus when somebody wishes and tries to be more proactive in adding this element of utility to it, the utility of that work automatically gets enhanced. With this increased or enhanced utility, the chances of his success become brighter and brighter which in turn wins the heart of the people... This is what success is all about. By making our life more useful, we can enhance its relevance.

For instance, in the days of floods, suppose, you helped a suffering family. But by doing so, what did you gain? – Did you get any money? You got nothing, No...?

You are forgetting perhaps. You, in fact, had gained a lot. Recapture that feeling of satisfaction when, due to your efforts, the family had got back their happiness. Remember readers, how happy you felt inside your heart, when you saw their happy faces. Really great! No amount of money, wealth, reward can adequately equate the satisfaction that you got out of the whole thing. More than a million dollar happiness. Will you not call it your success...?

Such precious moments add to the sweetness of our life, and these hundred small pleasures combine to make life joyful. But they give not only joy, they teach us too. These small happenings are really big happenings because they teach us to interact. They change our attitude to life. The first big change is that they change our mind-set, our attitude. We begin to give a message to ourselves – 'Oh I have to make my life useful, I can't lose it'.

In fact, it is not the number or quantum of happiness, but the very 'depth' of it that matters. It is intensity of the feeling of emotional involvement (compassion) that we develop, that matters.

Friends, compassion is that mother of all virtues. Compassion possesses the element of peace which can make our heart and mind stress-free and lighter. It can help us get over all the paradoxes, letting us not lose sight of our meaningful and relevant goal.

It must be remembered in this behalf that one who is compassionate to his own self, he alone can be compassionate to others.

It is not that one who has money, wealth and fame alone, is rich. The real wealthy is the man who is compassionate. The rest of the affluences are all vain. *Now... who will like that his life goes all vain? No body, perhaps no body!*

Come, let us carve out a place for ourselves too in this world of stars. Let us shine and brighten up our life and its successes. Let's give the world a new light with the virtues we have, so that the splendour of joy and happiness may keep our life glowing all the time...

Substance...

Pay attention to the following points :-

- I shall study and evaluate my abilities and capabilities closely and shall decide my objectives and the goal in accordance with them.
- I shall neither imitate others nor shall I run after other people's success. Instead, I shall carve out my own way.
- I can neither become as others are, nor can any other person become as I am. As such I shall try to become what specialties I am made of.
- I shall ever be a learner – learning from the success and failures of others. By doing so I shall keep on adding to my own success and reducing the failures.
- I am born to grow and prosper into a wholesome person. And as such I shall keep on enhancing the meaningfulness of my entity and shall at the same time keep enjoying the related process.
- I shall not compare myself with others, nor shall I drag my life after other's examples or by out of just being enamored of them.
- I shall keep my ideal before me, but I shall not make it the last word or the ultimate one. By doing so I shall go on getting into the limitless realm of my own capabilities.
- I shall cultivate my temper with the maximum possible virtues and shall develop and give due expression to my inner brilliance.
- For me success would be of supreme importance and I would not lose it at any cost.
- It shall ever be my endeavour to keep myself engaged in the achievement of success. For I know that if I am able to do so, other things would be automatically drawn in towards me.
- I shall enlighten my life with the light of compassion and shall brighten the whole world with its sparkle, spreading this light over the entire world.

Successful people go a step forward and pay attention to solutions

We first invite the problems

The whole thing starts when we try to give others those things which we don't have with us. This is the beginning of all the problems

The other day I was on tour, when I got a phone call from a very important doctor – 'Look, I want that milsef (a product) of yours. This is urgent. My son is leaving for China the day after tomorrow, I have to send milsef with him'.

The doctor had assigned this small job to me. He said that it was important.

I said – "Ok sir, it will be arranged". I had said this without thinking or making any effort first to confirm whether, I had the time with me for it at all. When I looked for it in my bag, I found that there was no "milsef" there. I suddenly got puzzled. Actually I was upset at the thought of my commitment and was not able to concentrate on work that I was doing. Suddenly in the midst of my work, I thought of taking the help of my fellow worker.

I at once found him and said – 'the certain doctor wants me to get for him a sample of 'milsef', 'could you arrange to send one for me? You may take the sample back in return from me. If I am able to give this sample to the doctor, I will be able to keep my word'. I said to him.

This fellow worker of mine agreed to do my work and after making a packet of the medicine he went to the courier and requested him to send this packet in time, saying – "It is to be sent at Sojat City address, will it reach to the party in time by the evening tomorrow?" The courier fellow said – "It will reach by the evening the day after, or may be the next day. There is no direct service to the place, so please think once again about giving it to me."

My friend rang me up soon explaining the whole situation. A little disappointed, I said – Ok, there is no point in sending it when it cannot reach in time. Please leave it."

This made me more worried I thought that if I was not able to keep my word, I could spoil my relations with the doctor. While I was still thinking all about it, I telephoned to a medical store, which was nearby this man's house. I explained to this 'new' medical man the whole thing brining him round to do my work that is to furnish me the medicine sample.

He listened to me carefully and said, "I will be able to give one by the day after tomorrow. In fact, my stock of this medicine finished only today. I am placing the order right now, as soon as I get the medicine, I will make it available to him."

I told this man also that it would be too late and thus there was no point in my bothering him. The thought, that the doctor would not be happy to hear all this was bothering me all this while.

In this way, I found myself caught up in a strange situation and the pity of it was that it was all my own doing. I was in a dilemma because I had not said a plane 'no' to the doctor. In fact, I realized then that it would have been much better if I had once checked up my stock before saying yes, then this situation would not have developed. In fact it was at my over-enthusiasm to tell him 'yes' that I had invited this trouble and here I was with a guilt in my mind and with no way out with me.

Now, if we look at this whole situation, we may come to the conclusion that sometimes we add to our problems ourselves by first inviting them and then to bother about finding solution thereof. In the way we spend our precious energy twice – first in creating or inviting problems and then getting rid of them... Is it a thoughtful approach?

Thoughtful people, instead, do not involve themselves in troubles. They always try to evade them. Although it is not easy in every situation to do so, because there are several problems to which we are not a party, but will by coming in contact with a certain set of outside situations, we cannot always escape from them. And in these situation sometimes in our over-enthusiasm may fall in the wrong track, do unwanted act or behave in an unbecoming manner.

In fact, we all wish that we make no mistakes – but no, since we are not living in a vacuum, to err or to create or fall a prey to problems is only too human a thing. The grass-root fact is that life has its own share of problems, of course ranging between negligible in case of some people, and very many in case of some others.

In fact, to make a mistake is not a problem. But to repeat the same mistake, to do it again – that is a big problem. Again, there are people who do not do things for fear of making mistakes. They won't do anything and obviously would not make any mistakes.

Persons who accept their problems, they become conscious and more aware of the problem. They do not worry about why problems are there in life, they instead try to find solutions of the problems they have.

Identifying the problem correctly – therein itself lies the solution

Most of our friends around are not worried because they have nothing to do; they are worried because before doing a 'work they try to 'find' problems in it. They tend to think that it is no use indulging themselves in things unnecessarily. And as it often happens, they keep tackling these imaginary problems and reach nowhere – a strange mind-set where there is 'no doing of things' and naturally no mistakes. Such people ultimately end up with no gains, no achievement, no acquisitions of their own, in life.

'Indeed there is no problem which is big enough to defy solutions'. Those who are of this mind-set do not fall apart even in the face of a problem. Instead, they forge ahead trying to find the solution thereof. In the process, they do make progress in their work and in due course, the problems tend to lose their gravity, and finally are left far behind.

But for all this, it is they who have first to identify the real problem and also what exactly is coming in the way of finding solutions. Otherwise, if one cannot identify his problem, how will he be able to find remedy thereof.

The moment we identify the problem, the task of finding its solutions become pretty easy. In this process the ideas in our mind go on becoming 'solution-oriented' rather than 'problem ridden'. In the process further, we do not cut ourselves away from the negative ideas, instead we tend to develop a completely neutral attitude. By getting into this non-thinking mode, we become more aware and conscious of the solution and keep on our concern for it. It is in such a state of mind that we come to get a suggestion of the solution.

It is in these suggestions that valuable solutions come to the fore. It is thus that the solutions keep on appearing and the problems keep on disappearing or receding. Thus solutions do not come from anywhere else, but from our own inside. And we share these solutions coming from within us and may find a solution to our problem.

While serving in a Company a certain young man felt that the real success does not lie merely in obtaining a job, but in lies in ameliorating the employment-problem of others and dwelling upon the problem, he felt that for removing unemployment, more and more industries will have to be set up and job opportunities created.

With five friends of his, he formed a company with an initial capacity of just rupees ten thousand. Starting from a meagre ten thousand rupees, the Company gradually picked up to become today a very successful one with business worth millions of rupees. The Company, at the same time, provides employment to thousands of people and to provide them further resources to march ahead on the path of progress. The whole world is enamoured of its success. The name of the Company is 'Infosys' – one of the world's most prestigious company, and the said young man is – N. R. Narain Murty.

As Narainmurty himself says at one place – "I consider myself as a Karmyogi – a person who not only thinks or discusses things, but also earnestly wishes and tries to translate them into action."

Great man do not run away from problems, they try instead, to make them run away or vanish. The past times and the present – both are a witness to this phenomenon that great men have always become great by fighting things through, by struggling hard, which leads us to formulate the moral that our attempts at solutions do not consume our energies, they, on the other hand, enhance them, as if we are further charged with them. We can move towards the solutions only by concentrating towards them. The more we work towards them, the more specialised in the field we become. The real solution of the problem lies in 'identifying' it.

Important thing in life is not 'how many problems we are having', but how many solutions we have got in order to do away with them. The better the solutions we adopt, the more our proximate we are to success.

Successful people are those who go beyond the problem.. to concentrate more on the solution.

Whenever a problem comes before us. We get worried and upset. We become stressful. 'I am caught in the web, what to do now?' and the result of this upsetting is that although we are in a position to find a remedy, we are not able to hit the nail on its head – the solution. Why does it happen so? It happens because we remain attentive to the problem only, and do not gather the courage even to think of the solution. The attention to the problem breeds more attention to it.

We should ordinarily evade problems in our life. It is better we keep off them. But if they have come and taken on us, then the only alternative with us is to solve them and let them not take the better of us. Once they have come, we should fight them out with all our might, we should then solve the problem and clear our way for our routine work and the consequent progress. If the problem has cropped up, we should treat it as a part of our work and then deal with it accordingly.

There are people who believe that if there is a problem, they are solutions also; If there are obstacles, there are ways to remove them too. With this mind-set they should be able to crack the problem like a search engine.

A search engine works and keeps things stress-free. Similar to it is our mind. When it is stress-free, it can think of bringing to light a proper solution. Thus the stress gets removed, and now comes the stage of and the thought of finding a solution. Now, we can be very natural with our work and we can try to work out the next step on the way to solution.

Come on, let us discuss this thing a little more detail – suppose while you are walking, a thorn pricks your foot. Blood oozes out at the same time, and you begin to feel the pinch and you nearly feel like crying. You get all upset.

Now, what will you do? Would you curse the thorn or you will curse yourself feeling guilty as to why you did not take care. You may even be grieving as to why the thorn pricked you out of all. You might also complain why people throw about the thorny things on the way. You might think of even putting a hard slap on the face of thorn. But what you need to think is – what will happen if we resort to all or one of these ways – Nothing! The broad moral we may draw with regard to problems in general is that they (problems) can end only by finding solutions there to and not by cursing them.

The fact of the matter is that the thorn has pricked your foot. Now the wisdom lies in getting a proper treatment done. The moment you start thinking about the treatment, you draw yourself out of the feeling of pain and begin to be more active towards its solution. The treatment and all other things related to it start happening. For instance, you may pick-up the thorn from the path and throw it far away so that it may not hurt others. You may even impress upon others that they may take due care while walking or you may even make others aware that it is not good to throw about thorns on the way.

By doing so you are put to a two way advantage – No 1, you forget the feeling of the pinch the thorn has caused, and No 2, you become more alert with regard to it and save yourself from trouble in future.

But if somebody does nothing and remains inactive even after such an episode, then the fellow himself is a problem and his inertness itself should be the big problem.

The persons who want to remove the problems from their way and go ahead on the path of progress are presumed to have understood them and taken upon themselves the task of removing them altogether. Such people, are able to successfully find solutions which prove productive. Thus, for such people no problem remains a problem, It turns at the end of the day, into a productive thing. Such people, again, become expert not only at identifying the problems but also at the solution-tracking process... This by itself is 'success'. Here one is, in fact, active and more concerned vis-à-vis the solution rather than the problem.

Always remember – successful people always go beyond the problems and pay more attention to solutions.

As our productivity goes up our problems get receded and as difficulties in the task seem to be getting solved, with each solution, a new energy seems to be taking birth and then we begin to wonder at our own self and say – 'Oh, I have done this!' – In this way we prepare ourselves for solution of even bigger problem.

To-day the scenario is that problems are rampant. We find them raising their heads anywhere and everywhere. But we also find that the brave and daring heroes do not give in to the problems. Rather, they make the problems give in to them. *It is thus, that we have to live – live with our heads high!*

Having talked about 'problems' at length, let us turn now, dear readers, to the solutions-aspect. We hand you over to the Solutions – part of the story so that removing the obstacles from the way, we may tread on and on, keeping our goal of success in mind...

Substance...

Pay attention to the following points :-

- I shall not invite unnecessary problems and shall be avoiding them as far as possible, thus saving my everyday life from troubles.
- Saving myself from being entangled in problems, I shall save my precious energy and shall employ it, instead, in constructive work.
- I shall learn from my own mistakes and shall avoid repeating them, thus making myself free from the fear of committing them.
- I shall identify my problems and accepting them, shall leave them to be dealt with by the due process of solution.
- I shall take my problems on to the zero stage – the stage of vacuity, thus enhancing my consicous of or awareness towards them. This will give rise in my mind to the inauguration of solutions. Guided by this I shall be able to do away with the problems altogether.
- I shall not turn my face away from problems, instead I shall endeavour and struggle to remove them from my way and overcome them forthwith.
- With the solution of the problems I shall put my feet into the vast area of possibilities, and in and while doing so, I shall be enhancing the dynamism of my energy.
- In my work, I shall regard the problems as a part of the game and shall continue to solve them by refusing to come under any stress.
- It shall be my endeavour to cure the problems instead of cursing them.
- I shall turn problems into production and thereby bring about far-reaching changes in other people's lives too.

Quality in itself is a source of publicity...

No Brand is sold, it is bought.

An intresting thing happened the other day when I went to buy a Baniyan (inner wear) at a nearby shop belonging to an acquaintance of mine. I told him that I wanted two Rupa Frontline Baniyans. He stopped for a while and then told me in a very low voice, I have got another 'very good brand' Baniyan. It is selling like anything these days. Shall I give you one from that lot?' he tried to explain the point very cleverly.

However, despite his explaining all that he wanted to, I was not convinced and I told him – 'Never mind, if you don't presently have the item, don't bother, I shall have it from some other place'.

A little annoyed he said ironically that he wondered if I wanted to wear a Baniyan or 'a brand'.

His oblique question did not deter me, nor convince me as I slipped out from the shop empty handed. What impact did this piece of conversation have in future? –Let it be shared and heard right here.

A few days later, I stepped in the same shop once again in order to buy some important things. As soon as the shop-keeper saw me, he at once spoke – 'Sir I have now got the Baniyan of the brand you wanted. Next time, please buy one from here itself.'

Superficially, we may find that most products or services are sold in the market and we go to the market to buy them, but the reality is somewhat different.

As a matter of fact, it is we who go to buy them, and that is why, they are available for sale. Thus it is the buyer who causes the sale of products. If there is no buyer, the product howsoever good, will lie unsold. This shows that the buyer is equally important as the seller. We may, therefore, conclude the funda that no brand is sold, it is bought.

The question then arises – why do we buy a thing at all? The answer is: Due to the presence of quality in that thing.

It is the quality that gives publicity to a thing.

As a seller, we should keep this thing in mind that it is not our duty just to make a product or to supply it. Instead, our job is to make or furnish such things as can fulfill the needs of others. If we make some product in a hurry without giving it due thought, we might end-up making a thing which does not satisfy the need of the people at all. Those who don't keep this thing in mind, suffer losses.

If we are making a thing, we are guided by the consideration of the wants or needs of the people. Plus, we also care to add *that* particular quality which the buyer expects to be there.

It is quite an old incident. We were almost about to reach Rohat, a small town in Pali District. My Manager said, 'Do you know Rohat is famous for its Kachories?' I said, "I don't know this, "But still we can just have a try." Then he said, "Then let's have a try". Saying this, he stopped the car in front of the famous Kachori shop.

I found that it was a very ordinary shop and there was a lot of rush in front of it. In fact the people were vying with each other to get their share of the sale first. I also followed the suit. Most of the people holding the currency notes in their hands in order to save time waited for their turn impatiently while the shopkeeper was all the time trying to pacify them by saying – 'Don't be too hasty, everybody will get his share as soon as I finish preparing it.'

But the buyers were in a mad hurry and they were frantically trying to draw the shopkeeper's attention – each buyer in his own way.

The shopkeeper however went on making the kachories in his own leisurely fashion. He was all the time so very casual and detached from the scene that he lifted his head up to look at the buyers after about 10 minutes, only when he had cooked one installment. And in no time he sold the whole lot. I also took my share of it and ate it right there saying, "Oh very very tasty indeed!"

The question here arises – why was the shopkeeper so unmindful of the buyers? And the answer is – because he did not want to make any hurry and compromise with the quality of the kachories he was making. The thought of making quality kachories was the upper most in his mind. That is why again that he had been able to maintain the quality for which his product – the kachories – were famous. Rush or no rush, he could never have made a sub-standard thing, only because people were in a hurry.

Supposing, he had overlooked the element of quality and made a far larger number of kachories and would have sold them to a large number of customers. It was quite possible for him to do so and in that case, his sale too would have been very good, but definitely people would not have got that much of taste for which the shop was famous. That would have told upon his sale as well as reputation.

A customer never visits a shop again if he is not satisfied and if the commodity or the service of the product does not fulfill his need and his expectations. A customer comes to eat kachori... not to eat the 'prestige' of the kachori.

It is one thing to attract customers for the first time to our selling-counter, but it is quite another to maintain the clientele. That would mean maintaining the quality or the standard of the product. A customer doesn't come again and again because of the fame, but he does so because of the quality of the product. Thus we can conclude that it is the quality that brings name to the product or the company or the shop, and mere prestige or fame of the shop does not necessarily bring quality.

Thus there is a direct relationship between quality and fame. Quality always treads ahead and the fame follows it. Those producers who are quality–conscious in respect of their product, are most likely to be able make their product a brand. The better the brand, the higher the fame.

Quality in itself is a source of publicity

Today, the situation is that the world has become a very big market. Therefore, it is true that publicity, advertisements and propaganda have become extremely important. For, our product may be very good but unless it reaches out to the people and unless they know about it, how would they buy it?

But we should always remember that it is one thing to attract the consumers or customers once, but it is quite another to keep them connected with our product continuously and over a long period, and they will keep connected only if they find quality there in the product. This implies that we may rely more on quality rather than on advertisement.

The reason is that the money spent on the overhead of advertisement can enhance the price of a product to a dangerous level – to a level that may prove to be a matter of loss instead of profit in terms of sale. If the rate or the price goes too high up, it may be that customers will not keep connected with us, and will become drop-outs.

When, appreciating this fact, we get to employ our energies in the making of useful products, this energy gets really reflected in our product and whosoever comes in contact with us and uses the product, he feels good about it and its usefulness or 'its performance', if we may say so. In fact, the product comes to have a direct contact with him and no wonder this contact gets further diversified and expanded. It is a stage, where, irrespective of somebody speaking about it or not speaking, it itself reaches out to speak volumes to others. Whosoever is happy with our product, he tells about it to others – thus tells the second to the third, the third to the fourth and so on... and the thing gets publicised. This publicity is automatic and continuous.

Mouth-publicity is one such tradition of publicity by which, in almost no expenses, the product reaches out to a long range of people. Why is that so? The answer is simple – if the quality of the product is very good, then it – the quality itself – becomes the first-hand experience of the people and the subject matter of their talk.

But how long does it last? ... Until the time we keep ourselves fully dedicated to our work. The moment we are a little slack, some other product finds an empty space to make it its own place. Had it not been so, we would have been using even today, such of those things as were in vogue hundreds of years ago, and as are in vogue in our day-to-day life even today. This leads us to conclude that it is not the product, but its quality that is always in the news. Quality lasts, the product may keep changing. Poorer quality thus gets lagged behind and the better quality forges ahead.

Whatever equipments or products are available today, they had first taken shape in the mind of a successful person – whether it be a TV or a refrigerator or a car or a mobile or a robot or computer – all of these are the products of some creative people's mind.

Any creative idea first takes birth in the mind. No object can come to get an external shape unless it has been got first composed in somebody's mind. A thing can acquire an external or a constructed form only after it has first passed through the corridor of man's insight. In the course of this process, imagination of the creator comes into play and helps to culminate it into the final creation. Thus in this process the composition takes place first, and the production follows the suit.

So if we forget 'the base of the composition' and directly involve ourselves in 'the process of production', we lose the systemic thread and in the over-involvement with the process, we tend to care less for the product's quality-aspect. By imposing too many restrictions on the composition, the artist loses his hold on the product. And the whole effort tends to create a distance between the maker, and his creative instinct, on the one hand, and the product on the other.

However, by being creative and productive, we become free of all the impositions, and this freedom results in production or creation of something, which directly touches the heart. Therefore, we should render our production on the basis of our composition and should not base our composition on production.

'Composition and creativity' is what takes birth inside, and what has been 'constructed' appears outside.

There are two kinds of people in our world. The first kind is those who look outside for the fulfillment of their needs. They pay certain price for getting for themselves certain things or equipment. When they have got the equipment or the things, they put the latter to use, and in this way they become 'Consumers'.

The other kind of people are those who identify needs of the consumers and create the things for their need. Thus they become 'producers'. When they become producers, they get or realise the price of their product from their users. In the satisfaction of the needs of the consumers lies their success. In this way these people become what are called industrialists.

Ordinarily being a consumer is easy and becoming an industrialist is difficult. But in the long run those persons alone can earn a brand-name, who have a highly developed sense of industry (industrial acumen) on the basis of which, they can cater to the needs of the consumers for a long time. This doesn't mean that the consumers have no relevance or identity in the matter. But it may be appreciated that if there is no industrial effort, the existence or non-existence of the consumers would become meaningless. In other words, consumers draw their relevance from the industrial effort put in the thing.

In fact, any composition or creative effort is a means of expressing ourself, expressing our personality. It gives a fulfillment to our urge of self-expression. When we are constructive or creative, we manifest our own selves and thus are able to enjoy the whole process, which, passing via composition, turns into production. Through such an effort, we are able to provide the best quality to the product.

A great composer or a creator is a person who is humble in his act of composition and doesn't do anything forcibly. He completes his task with humility. When a creator is conscious of this aspect, his attention is not distracted by other things and he, whole-heatedly and full-fledgely, devotes himself to creativity or constructivity alone. And it is then that he is able to bring out the best in his composition and to give expression to his idea in terms of what he really desires. When it is so, the effort and the product will include his heart and soul therein. The product thus will also be able to carve out a place in the hearts of the people... This is 'success'. What else is success? – By being aware of what the subject-matter and the composition really demands, we can accordingly turn out a quality product.

Always remember – the creative rises from inside, and the thing manufactured or the product formed acquires appearance outside.

The products of the success, work as a magnet and draw the people's attention towards them. People on their part get drawn to them and enjoy the services rendered by them.

Although many of our friends change the packing and make it appear very attractive, but they put the material therein of a very low quality, and forget that by changing the packing, the material inside doesn't get changed. Packing is throwable and will be thrown out but the thing inside is supposed to be put to use. The reality will come out when we actually use the inside-thing, like we always eat the gulab jamuns and not the packing thereof.

It is true that the needs of the people change with the times but it is equally true that our quality and power of being constructive and creative always remains intact, and does not get lost. By being in touch with the constructiveness and reality we can develop products that are in tune with the times. By doing so, we will be rightly employing our time in the production of a more important thing – *the production of joy and happiness.*

Come, let us pay particular attention to those compositions which are currently our need. The idea is that we may set ourselves prepare high-quality products to meet these needs, and along with making them available to those who need, we can get into the 'action-mode' once again to fulfil the new needs...

Substance...

Pay attention to the following points :-

- The thing that I want to have is bound to become available to me. This rule is applicable to me and to all other people equally.
- My creation is the result and reflection of my proficiency – the quality of ability that I posses. As such I will always count on my own quality by virtue of which my compositions will get their due appreciation and preference.
- My real and basic work would be to produce such quality goods that may satisfy and fulfil the needs or wishes of the people using or buying them. I shall thus present my products with the aforesaid specific aim in view.
- My qualities would bring me fame and due to my fame, my product would get great encouragement and a boost-up. In this way my products are bound to become so very sought after.
- I shall decide the criteria of my quality myself without being influenced by any outside factors and shall at no cost make any compromises in this behalf.
- People would utilise my quality products and not my fame. As such it would be my endeavour to enhance the quality of my product further. This would bring me fame automatically.
- I shall of course take the help of advertisement and publicity, but not being wholly dependent upon them, I shall see that my production cost does not get too high.
- I shall spend my resources on quality, and thus shall be producing things keeping in view the maximum benefit of the users.
- The high level of quality would become the talk of the town and this will further go on to enhance people's interest in my product. My product thus would always hit the headlines of the newspapers and will constantly remain in lime light.
- I shall create things rendering their composition as the very crux of my production-activity and shall leave the production-process to follow the composition.

The Possibilities of Being Successful Are Always Open...

There is nothing in the world that is impossible.

Whenever we come across some disorderliness, some incompatibility or some inequality, we leave it at what it is, without making any effort or doing anything to correct the thing. This happens because we know that this is ultimately going to happen the same way again. And in this vein we wrongly, though helplessly, tend to take, treat and accept even the wrong activities as normal and do not do anything about them. By falling a prey to this tendency we serve to encourage the wrong things to be repeated. This attitude and approach make our life less dignified. By taking our life off the standards of morality, we cannot hope to raise the possibilities of success.

The truth is that our upliftment lies only in working for upliftment. It is when we adopt a positive attitude like this that we are able to stand against the opposing forces coming in the way of our upliftment and progress in life. Thankfully, it is in the wake of such situations that the possibilities of failure seem to get vanished, and those of upliftment and improvement get boosted up and are seen rising.

Mahatma Gandhi studied Law and became a barrister. It is common knowledge (vide his Autobiography) that once he had to go to South Africa in order to conduct a case. During one of his railway journeys he encountered an ugly incident. It was a bitter experience for him. Gandhiji had duly bought the ticket and had sat in a compartment in which all the occupants were white people. They did not like Gandhiji's taking a seat in the said compartment and sitting with them. They were so inconsiderate that they lifted him up and bodily threw him out of the compartment.

Gandhiji was shocked and disillusioned. It was a traumatic experience. It shook him from his very inner self. But he was not going to take this humiliation lying down. He resolved to take up in his hand the mission of correcting the things, and we all know, it was his effort on account of which, things subsequently came to be improved.

The story of the rest of his life is the story, we all know, of his active participation in public life there in South Africa, where while leading this public life he undertook and accomplished many tasks which made an unprecedented impact and brought about positive changes in the people's life there. He began to enjoy this kind of work relating to public life and this sense of enjoyment brought more successes to him, and with each success the area of his activities grew larger. Thereafter he got associated with the Freedom movement of India and gave it tremendous impetus, and his tormented soul did not rest for a moment even, until the country, through his non-violent revolution, got the much-coveted freedom from the British rule.

Can one dare to undertake such a great and huge task without having a faith in its success? – Can such a degree of strife be ventured into without having an understanding of the possibilities entailed therein? – The answer obviously would be – No.

Yes, of course, every one of us may not be able to do such a big thing, but we can at least care to stop such of the activities which are down-right anti-social and immoral, thereby enhancing the possibilities of saving us from the dangers of adverse forces that lie in the way of raising the moral and material standards of us including our's standard of living.

Whenever we come across some incongruity, we should not take it lightly or casually, discarding the idea of doing something about it –'Everything is over, nothing can be done now' : Instead of reacting like this, our approach should be : 'All is not over yet, much can be done even now'. It is a psychological fact that the moment we think in these terms, our own mind-set changes, and we really begin to feel that what we are proposing to do is possible. With this changed mind-set, our faith in our own self gets strengthened, and we are charged physically and mentally to such an extent that we suddenly become passionately dynamic and end up only at cracking the possibility we were seeking to crack.

'Impossibility' is a word which is found in the dictionary of those people who do not want to do anything. As against them, there are persons who are aware of their aims and goals and who, thereby, may connect themselves with the thoughts of making even the impossible things possible, and when we have this mindset, the ghost of the negative attitude of our belief in the impossible automatically vanishes.

One who is interested in being successful, finds possibility in every thing, because he is a believer in the dictum that 'impossible is a word which is there in the dictionary of fools'. But in the case of one who is all the time running away from success, how can we notice any possibility, –even if it is there in him?

Those who have in their mind the thoughts of the possibility of getting over the crisis will certainly be able to get over it and achieve success.

Even a fall has the seeds of the possibility of rise.

If, once a man gets broken, gets shattered or suffers a fall, it does not mean that he is doomed forever. For no state in this life stays for ever. Change is the law of Nature. In life, changes take place frequently, so much so that change becomes a regular feature and a permanent part of our life. Adversities coming in our life should be treated in the same way, thinking that they are just short-time or temporary guests, so that we may not suffer a back-slide or down-fall, and may keep ourselves connected with progress.

If we look at the events that took place in the life of great men of the past and the present, we will find that each one of them had suffered failures in life and each one of them found out ways of coming out of them, and finally they came out successful.

Take the example of a mango tree having been felled on having got rotten. But we cannot think or take it that it is all over with the tree, for the simple reason that a new tree out of it can still grow or be grown in future. But it is possible only when we put its mango seed in a fertile spot of land. It may be that the new seeds turn out to be giving still larger number of mangoes. This can happen and cannot be ruled out. In this way the earlier adverse situations can be covered up by the newly developed situations and we can begin to live life afresh and with redoubled energy and fervor, zeal and passion.

In fact, even in the mindset of a fall, possibility of rise is often present. Only we are not able to recognize it. Those who can apprehend these possibilities, have yet another chance to rise, but those who can not apprehend, would be deprived of success despite the presence of possibilities.

There came a time when the India's economy was at the lowest ebb. Nobody was prepared even to give it loan. The reserves of foreign currency in the country's treasury were almost negligible. The country in these circumstances was forced to mortgage its gold. But despite this acute economic crisis, a ray of hope could still be seen. There was a chance, though remote, of coming out of this uncharitable situation.

In a debacle like this, Dr. Manmohan Singh was made to take over as the Finance Minister. He had just retired from the government job at that time and was having a relaxed time. Dr. Manmohan took a stock of the possibilities of some new economic reforms being launched and in the same strain proposed a new chain of economic reforms which kept the people amazed. The economy of the India got on to the line once again, and Dr. Singh began to be recognised as a world-famous Finance Minister of rare acumen.

In his statement he express this thought in his own manner – "I feel that the present growth rate of 8% can not only be maintained but even can be extended too to 10% as the goal of the growth rate of economic development."

In fact, those who wish to simply govern others, they can neither be necessarily really successful themselves, nor can they be particular in regard to the success of others, because theirs is a limited agenda, namely, that of administration or governance, with no concern for exploring newer possibilities of welfare and with development occupying only a back-seat. Their vision, mind-set, attitude, attention concern and the consequent approach is usually altogether different.

In a governance-oriented agenda, the imposition of the will of the administration is the supreme-most factor, irrespective of all other considerations. It has a stringent, authoritarian, undemocratic approach in which there is little room for considerations of development, welfare, practicality, humanitarian elements, or for development or success of others.

The second approach is usually a democratic, broad-visioned, participative, coooperative, human and liberal approach in which chances of possibilities of and the concern for the people's successes are considerably marked and their development and success occupy a prime seat on the agenda.

In this second approach – called the liberal approach – one automatically gets to develop greater possibilities of success. This approach mainly addresses itself to the agenda of development, welfare and success.

Where there is liberal approach, the chances of development are stronger

When we are liberal, our approach to our own self broadens. In a situation like this, we become aware of all those possibilities which are there inside us. On the basis of the presence of these possibilities, we become active and serious and confident towards the achievement of those goals which we have been wishing to attain. The awareness of the presence of possibilities prevents us from lapsing into lethargy or from getting dull or inactive or lazy.

As per a report, when Mukesh Ambani decided to take command of the Reliance Industries, the volume of their business was around Rs. 100 crores. Now the company has crossed over this line to an extent of lacs of crores. In doing all this Mukesh Ambani has only followed the footprints of his father and has extended his work. This happened only because of his working devotedly for those limitless 'possibilities', the 'creation or generation' of which, had been the summon bonum of his family's industrial effort. Mukesh Ambani measures 'successes' in terms of 'possibilities or potentialities'.

Mukesh Ambani speaks of his dreams. – "Not millions of 'people' but millions of 'possibilities', each person being a possibility unto himself".

Possibilities is like a light lodged in our minds which shows us the path even in the darkest of darkness, provided we keep the switch of this light on. Obviously, if we keep the switch always off, and keep our mind-set closed, we might stray away from our path supposed to lead us to our destination.

The Tsunami's monstrous waves had caused such a devastation, had wrought such a havoc in the world! While the tempestuous sea was raging, Rijal Shahputra of Indonesia was doing the clearing of a mosque. A gush of the raging waters made Rijal its victim and whisked him away in its swaying waters. Even in such a tender situation, Rijal kept up all the effort to survive at his command. After being 'flooded' over along the waves and the tempestuous currents of water, he was almost at the point of giving up. He found himself surrounded by hundreds of corpses all around. Even amidst such an adverse situation he did not give up and kept looking for the possibilities of survival.

A huge palm tree served as an agent of rescue. He climbed it on and passed some most difficult days of his life. It was a grim struggle for survival. He survived himself on the coconuts flowing in the ocean and quenched his thirst by drinking salty water of the sea. He, however, kept shouting intermittently for help, and lo! His effort proved fruitful. A certain passing ship took him out of waters after he had been swayed and swept away for about 160 kilometers from Banda Eih! He was taken to a hospital forthwith. After recouping from his weakness, he was able to lead a normal healthy life again. The point here is that the fellow survived because of the fact that he did not leave his hold on the collar of possibilities until the last possible minute.

In fact, where there is open-mindedness, broad-mindedness and receptivity, there are greater possibilities of one's development, because we do not sit there with a closed frame of mind. There is greater exposure. There the doors are open for new possibilities. And we are ready to welcome them. This is what is known as a liberal attitude. Thus when we are liberal we do not get weakened, we come out, in fact, stronger. It is this strength which serves as an aid or a help to us for attaining our coveted goal - Success.

While grappling with realities, we usually keep ourselves engaged in testing or having a foretaste of the possibilities. In the process our chances of forging ahead are automatically kept up.

The possibility of success always remains open.

Whether it be our field of work or personal life or some objective of life or some other affair, it is usually our tendency to stop after a certain phase and to think : (that) 'well, it is enough; now we do not have to have more'. With this mode of thought we, as it were, put a lock on the rest of the possibilities and assume a posture of inaction. This is suicidal. It is strangulation of our progress. We are alive and yet have no life of ours. We are in a position to do and act, yet we are in a state of inaction, literally handing ourself over to inaction. This is putting a lock on our own self.

This is the kind of situation wherein a bird shuts itself up inside a cage, with door of the cage kept open. The bird is fluttering its wings, but does not try to get out of the cage, why this? – The reason is that the bird instead of exploring the possibilities of coming out, engages itself in looking for its justification for keeping itself shut in.

Thus to stop thinking in terms of future plans or of possibilities, entails two possible reasons : First – we seem to think that we have earned enough and therefore there is no need to earn any more. Influenced by this thought we propose passing the time idly, doing nothing. Second – we begin to feel that the count-down of life has begun and therefore not much can be done and therefore it is useless to try to do anything. Thinking in this mode, we began to just exist and pass off the rest of the days most unproductively.

If we really observe carefully, we come to find that every phase (of life) has its own amazing features. When we consider those amazing features, the reasons for the 'end of the possibilities' automatically vanish from the scene, and new avenues of what is still possible, are opened. Here then we come to realize that the time that is past is no time at all; the goal-post that stops us from achieving the goal is no goal-post at all; the age that stops us from active life is no age at all. In other words, neither time, nor obstacles, nor age, can come in our way of doing what we still can and want to do. In still other words, we still have a whole set of flood-gates of possibilities open, and the doors of possibilities are not closed on us. At such a stage we recast, redefine or redesign our aims and get and remain connected with those moments that lend us joy and happiness, which ultimately is our aim in life. This is success... By keeping the possibilities open, we can achieve the thing called success.

Always remember – possibilities of success are always open for us... Having thought in this mode, many of our friends never get retired, for even at this stage they are more worried for their goals rather than for their age or their handicaps owing to age. They find some new role for themselves in every phase and at any age. Age does not wither them, they overpower and influence their age itself.

The messiaha for those who are in agony – Mother Teressa – the embodiment of human service, once found a woman on the roadside. Her body was being nibbled at by mice and causing her more hurt. People saw the woman with great disgust and passed by. Mother Teressa took charge of this helpless woman and served her, and after this woman breathed her last, Mother Teressa vowed that she shall not let any helpless person in agony die on the road like that, and later on, this itself became Mother Teressa's mission in life. And she remained committed to this mission of hers till the end of her life.

If we have an inclination towards a busy and dynamic life, the possibilities of success is sure to be there with us at any stage, any phase and at any age. For, the possibility of success does not die until we allow it to die. Till we are alive, the potential or the possibilities inside us will remain alive to fetch us our share of success. Therefore, we should make the following dictum our guideline – *'There is so much always possible – at all times and each time, at any stage or at any age'.*

Come then, come with our arms open to embrace these possibilities so that the energy and vibrations flowing from them may get infused in us, causing the stream of happiness and joy in life to run unobstructed, unhindered, continuously and incessantly...

Substance...

Pay attention to the following points :-

- Disorder, discordance and inequality – I shall wilfully contribute to participate in any attempt made at correcting all these evils.
- I shall always work keeping in mind the consideration of progress and upliftment. I shall render the journey of life into an upbeating stance.
- Nothing is impossible and everything is possible – I shall start with this assumption and try to be on a look-out for every possibility and shall keep myself constantly engaged in this search.
- I shall not give up in the face of a possible defeat, and instead, shall look at the defeat as yet another opening for an opportunity, and it is with this approach in mind that I shall respond to the situations.
- I shall treat adversity or obstacles as passing phases of life and shall be thus ever looking forward to possibilities of progress, leaving my sense of pessimism far behind.
- I shall always pin my faith on the policy of human development, prosperity and welfare, and for which ideal, I shall keep myself open to and connected with the infinite and vast world of possibilities.
- I shall adopt a liberal approach to people, things and thoughts and life and shall behave with others liberally, keeping myself prepared for moulding and refining my personality or enriching it accordingly.
- Along with the realities I shall keep testing the oncoming possibilities and so soon I am assured of the chances of progress therein, I shall break my inertia and get on to become dynamic.
- I shall always be keeping an eye on my own amazing excellences and peculiarities, and shall be deciding upon my new role in the light thereof.
- I shall keep the possibilities of leading a liberal, as well as wholesome life open – a life full of thrill and excitement – full to their brim.

Our desires get strength from our will-power

Need is one, desires are many.

One day a little child asked his father for certain toys. His father took him to a very big toy shop of the place. As soon as they entered the shop, the child saw this huge collection of toys. He was just perplexed desiring to have all those toys which caught his fancy. He picked a lot many toys. His father tried to argue with him and say that it was pointless to have so many toys at one time because he won't be able to play with all of them at the same time. The child did not understand the implication of the money that the whole transaction involved. The father and son, finally, returned with a whole basket full of toys. And no sooner had they reached home than the child posed the big question – 'Which toy am I to play with, first of all?'

In fact, our mind at a given point of time can concentrate only on one point. Thus there may be lot many desires in our mind, but we can not fulfill them all at the same time. And despite this, if we try to do so, we are most likely to get confused and stand in a fix in deciding as to which desire or wish to be attempted to fulfill first and which to put off and to be attended to later.

In fact, there is a difference between 'needs' and 'desires'. Needs can be duly fulfilled, but unrestricted and uncontrolled desires can not be fulfilled. For, as already said in the beginning – 'need is one, desires are many' and the danger is that every desire will like to take the status of a need.

The obvious question that comes up is – Can we not control our desires? The answer would be – 'Yes..., we can, but for this it is important that we decide upon the desires in question with reference to the priority of our need. By doing this, the desire will draw its justification from the need, rather than the need justifying itself in terms of or in accordance with the desire... Of course, if we attach or assign a certain goal to a desire, we might be able to do so, but not otherwise. In this way every desire can take the shape of a need.

Imagine for a moment... if the father and the son in the 'toy' story had pre-decided to buy an aeroplane, then their task would have become much easier. No doubt the huge collection of toys would have been there as usual, but then the child would have concentrated on his object of desire, namely, the aeroplane, and would not have frittered away his concentration and energy on other objects unnecessarily.

Desires influence our life in a very strange and curious way. They crop up in our mind and consciousness so innocently and unawares that we do not recognise them until a point comes where these desires assume a dangerous level and when we hear this danger-alarm, it has become perhaps too late, as we have already fallen a prey to a whole lot of the said unrestrained and untamed desires.

Uncontrolled desires are like a horse with no reins. If you ride it roughshod it can tumble you down with a force that can shatter your existence and leave you unfit or incapable of nursing any further desires.

Whereas the reality is that our effort ought to 'fulfill' our desires and not to 'finish' them.

Only valid desires entail success and invalid desires only lead to failure.

A neat and clean house to live in, pure, disease-free water to drink, an appropriate job for adequate financial stability, means and facilities for our physical comfort and well-being, and use and adoption of techniques seeking to make life comfortable and developed – these are some of our basic desires today. I am no prude and so hold the view that we may include these basic desires in our list of healthy desires and to seek to fulfill them. It is no crime to include them in the list, I would even go a step further and hold that the desire to lead a healthy and prosperous life is our moral right. But we should remember, at the same time, that to acquire and possess, to grab and collect things beyond our needs is not justified. The desire to 'have more' is unwarranted. All sins begin with this desire.

Although every wish of ours whether if be valid or not valid... gets fulfilled as a result of our running about frantically to acquire the means to satisfy it. But the truth is that the real success lies only in the fulfillment of valid needs and the seeds of failure can be found soon, from the very beginning, in the case of invalid or unjustified needs.

For instance, when we are hungry, to crave for food and to get nourishing food is a need of ours. By eating it we get the necessary energy and we feel good and happy. But who can help the kind of person who suffers from over-eating or desiring to eat more after he has eaten to his full need and his stomach is already full? No doubt many of us do all this, but then they invite diseases and ailments and in the process they not only obtain no energy from food, but lose much of whatever is left. It is the finding of many expert-reports that those who eat more are more prone to disease and death.

The reality is that we can make use of a thing to the extent we need it. Any excessive use after that point tends to upset and interfere with our goal. For instance, ordinarily we need only one room to sleep in. Now knowing this full well somebody constructs 10 to 12 big bungalows. Now one wonders if that fellow will change his place of sleep every one hour? Or will he change his bungalow every next hour and go to the other bungalow of his and sleep there every now and then. Oh yes, one can do so, if one likes, but in that case he will not get sleep at all. Sleep will defy him.

The truth of all truths is that to sleep one needs just about 3 x 6 feet of space. And then whether any additional space exits or does not exist there, is just immaterial, making no difference whatever to our chances of sleep!

To collect things without need or use and just to make a show of them is not just theft or robbery, it is snobbery.

The basic reason behind most of our failures is nothing else than our unbalanced desires. Unbalanced desires upset our mind, cause panic, and by our remaining away from successes, make us despondent, and we thus pass the rest of our life in the dark shadows of despondency. The fault of all this does not lie with the wrong desires themselves, but with us our adopting the said wrong desires.

Some of our friends often advise that one should not be ambitious. Their argument is that invariably the ambitions become the cause of problems. But they forget that if we do not have any ambition, what would we work for? Had the successful people not been ambitious, the world would not have made such tremendous progress!

In fact, ambition does not serve to put an end to success. On the other hand it rennovates it. Therefore, it would be better to say that the cause of our troubles are not ambitions as such, but our invalid and unjustified desires. It is they who weaken us, not the ambitions.

It is not difficult to understand what our need is, but our problem is that we tend to include other's needs too in our needs led by our desire to amass as much wealth as possible, while others are deprived of it. This causes a big gulf between those who are 'haves' and those who are 'have nots'. Some people get extremely rich, others get poorer as they have negligible wealth. It is this imbalance in distribution of wealth that causes all the misery and unhappiness. If we can correct this mechanism of imbalance we will be able to cause more balanced distribution. That is why ambitious people can not be allowed to sit at home doing nothing. They need to work their hardest.

Those who are ambitious and more powerful, and able, can use their skills to help those others who are backward. By doing so the ambitious people themselves become stronger. The more they go on to share their skills with others, the more important and respected they become.

History says that those persons who have utilised or consumed things have not been respected so much, as those who have distributed things the most.

The more insistent or keen you become, the more strong-willed you become.

The strong will for success makes your wishes strong.

This is a well-known truth of life that every one wants to come out of troubles and wants to get success and become prosperous. We all wish that we take in hand such tasks as lead us towards a happy and peaceful life. It is, therefore, important that we ignite in ourselves a fire that may impel us to always remain active and remain in action.

The 'fire' referred to here is not the kind of one that 'burns' us, but the one that puts additional heat in our capacities to make them pucca, so that we may be impelled to stick to our goal in life and to continue to pursue the task that we are fond of, till our last breath, till the said fire gets put out.

A certain child growing up to be a young guy was inflicted with heart-trouble. The doctors, after examining him reported that his case was incurable and anything could happen any time. But the fellow wanted to 'live'. The strong streak of will power rising in him prepared him mentally to direct all his efforts in the task of curing himself of the ailment. He concentrated all his attention towards finding and applying alternative remedies for curing his heart-trouble. He changed his food habits and daily life style. Added to this was his will power and he began to get well, and in course of time, he became completely well.

Whatever the world might say, the fellow, by sheer dint of his will power was able to grapple with death's tardy hand, and by putting his life on the right lines managed to live and live well. Later, this man became a great writer and wrote a large number of books giving the readers a deep insight. As a gift this instance that I have taken from a magazine, gives us the moral that the will-power-to-be-successful puts a cutting edge on to our desires, on the basis of which we can work wonders in the field of our interest and choice.

This was Nelson Mandela's example. It was his sheer will-power that he took up a cause like that of the apartheid and made it his mission of life. For this he had to remain behind the bars of prison for a period which was the most precious phase of his life. He continued to pursue his programme and mission while still in jail. Ultimately, it is will-power that took the better of him and he kept stuck up to his mission. He pursued it do its hilt and ultimately the evil of the apartheid - the discrimination between white and black - the discrimination based on colour - in the South Africa, came to an end.

The leader of and from the masses like Anna Hazare lately have risen with his war against corruption. He and his team is up-in-arms against this cancerous disease which has been eating the very vitals of the nation. This is an issue on which the vested interests had tried to hackle him, weaken him, break his back, but no, his will-power is still keeping him in good stead and that's why the relevance of the mission of this man of the masses is still intact, thanks to his will-power. A person's will-power never weakens him, on the other hand, it uproots every evil, every weakness. As Anna Hazare states at one place – 'Your will-power should be that strong as may motivate you to struggle until your last breath'.

The desire to which we are deeply attached, later on becomes our ardent passion. The more we nurse and nurture this desire, the stronger it gets on to be.

Any desire of ours will get strength from our will-power alone.

If we just view the inside of our own self, we find that there are heaps of desires waiting to be fulfilled or realised, but if we were to look for the related will-power inside us, we would find that it (the will power) happens to be rather inactivated or sluggish. The reason is not that we lack in will-power, but it is that we ourselves tend *to be slow to activate it*. In a situation like this, despite the fact that we have our desires, yet they do not get fulfilled or realized.

There can be possibly two reasons for this. The first being that we do not get fully committed to fulfill it and the desire in issue gets vanished after some time. For instance, a certain person who want to become an engineer, but does not work for it whole-heartedly and in a committed fashion. That's why he just misses becoming an engineer. Secondly, we in the depth of our heart may be entertaining certain specific desires, whereas the atmosphere outside, around us, may impel us to entertain desires that are different. Thus we keep oscillating between these two and do not come to belong to either. For instance, a person has a deep desire to be a photographer but when he is influenced by the external atmosphere, he changes his decision and now, wants to become an engineer. Ultimately he is able to become fully neither a photographer, nor an engineer.

By respecting our own desire fully, we can see it getting fulfilled. By doing so, we become active in regard to our real desires which are originally there in our nature. Along with this, our inner powers get engaged in seeking support and to make it stronger. By this process our desire gets on to become a sort of strong will-power. And thus by remaining attached with it, we may realise our desired objectives... This is success. By making our desires powerful, we can get success in terms of realisation of our desired goals.

Always remember – any desire of ours will get strength from our will-power.

There was a certain mechanic. He had lost both of his hands in a surgical operation by doctors as a sequel to an accident. He became completely handicapped. He could not now do the work of a mechanic of scooters, etc. His daughter had been watching him do the mechanical work ever since her childhood. In fact, she had remained amidst that atmosphere all along. She could not see her father's miserable state of disability, at the same time. Experiencing a sense of great agony, she vowed, then, to help thousands of such other handicapped (besides her father) who had lost their hands.

She took to this work with great passion. She applied her mind in making and setting new parts of the machinery of scooters. She strived and strived and lo! she got success at last. But what success? She was able to manufacture such a scooter that could be driven by legs and feet. Her father's joy knew no bounds, because now he could drive his scooter with the help of his legs.

We feel like paying all the respect in the world, from the very bottom of our hearts to such daring people like her for her passionate desire to do such challenging things.

It lies, then, in our hands whether to pursue a desire or not to do so. No desires will get fulfilled automatically, we have to do something, welcome and adopt them. Being conscious of this power of ours, we may make any desire powerful, or else we may choose to make it powerless. It will all depend on us. Having realised this, we may now be prompted to say – *'The time has now come, we can do a lot in this field too.'*

Come on, Sir, let us give shelter to such of our desires which may help us in making our life real dignified, so that in making them strong, we may make our own life stronger...

Substance...

Pay attention to the following points :-

- I shall refuse to be dazzled by the glamour of desires; instead I shall be paying due attention to the fulfilment of my needs.
- I shall nurse my desires in accordance with my needs and not the other way round.
- I shall define my desires in terms of specific objectives and shall see that all my efforts are directed to the fulfilment of the said desires.
- Successful life and happy living is my moral right and I shall ever strive to take to activities relevant to the realisation of the said moral right.
- I shall, in my race of desires, include only valid desires and shall be keeping myself off the unreasonable, unwarranted and invalid desires.
- While pursuing and fulfilling my valid desires, I shall keep happy and cheerful and shall not lose my head i.e. shall keep my mental poise intact and mental energy in balance.
- I shall be ambitious, have an ambitious mind-set and with this mindset I shall address myself to the task of keeping the evolution of humanity on the right channels.
- I shall be adamant on seeking and attaining success and in the process I shall be making my will-power to act, strong.
- I shall nurse my will-power with due care and enhance its strength and activeness sufficient enough be capable of attaining the objectives already specified.
- I shall keep myself aware of common good and shall for achieving common good, employ the cutting edge of my will-power to the desired extent and intensity thereof.

Our fate is a reality – our reality, rather than a surprise

Why does it happen like this?

In our day-to-day life some strange things keep on happening, but there do happen certain incidents or events which compel us to reflect upon and say – 'Why does or did it happen like this'?

Like in everybody's life, in my life too, there happened so many things which cannot be forgotten. I have picked up three of these many events which I would like to share with you.

First – the other day I had been doing some work in connection with the preparation of necessary documents of my niece's application form. I was in the Collectorate premises and we had practically prepared all documents. Only the typing and attestation of one document was left to be done. I went to the typist. At that point of time only Rs. 40/- were left in my pocket. Referring to the typing work, I asked the fellow how much it would cost – 'Rs 30/- in all', answered the typist, obviously busy with the thought of this new piece of work.

Incidentally and rather casually, I asked – 'How much the notary-fellow would charge for this?' He readily answered – Please go to that Arora guy sitting under the tree. He will do it for Rs. 25/-'. This was an uninvited suggestion.

With one hand over my pocket, I got a little worried. While I was still lost in the thought : How shall I manage the rest of the work in Rs. 10/-, I mechanically reached the 'Notary-fellow under the tree'. I put up the Certificate in question before him, telling him that it was to be attested.

I kept standing there while he read the Certificate and put his seal thereon and signing it he said – No matter, you may pay Rs. 15/- later on when you come here next time. At least the work of this 'child' will not be held up now, I suppose.

I was surprised at the whole thing. I reflected and wondered without my telling him any thing, how could he think of the dilemma I was in and how on earth did he decide to proceed to help me out!

Second – It was quite dark, pitch-dark, I suppose. It was already quite late by then. Vehicles? There were hardly any vehicles on the road. I was coming back home after leaving a relative of mine at his house. Then I saw a man on the road. He was walking with difficulty as the things he was carrying were heavy.

I stopped my motorbike and offered him lift telling him that I was going in the same direction and I would drop him. He heard me and stopping for a while said – 'Don't you worry about me. I shall walk down, you may please proceed!'

Seeing his pitiable condition, I told him not to be too obstinate or insistent and that he would not be getting any rickshaw there. I was going that side only and so he should not make it such an issue and may sit behind me. Heaving a deep sigh, he looked into my eyes intensely –'Haven't I told you that I am not interested in getting a lift. You better go, your way and I, go mine'. And with this I proceeded on my way.

All the way through I wondered and thought why he was not ready to accept my offer of help despite my request!

Third – One day I was going to my village. My family was with me. My brother was driving the car. Soon after we were out of the outskirts of the city. He increased the speed of the car. We may have gone about 25 to 30 kms then suddenly he realised that a heap of concrete lay in front of us and there was a temporary way on the side. As he turned the car with a jolt to one side, the car skipped downwards and, in order to control the speed when my brother applied the break, he was shocked to realize that the brakes of the car had failed. He shouted loud to announce that the brakes had failed. We were all flabbergasted as he accelerated the car with the same speed and managed to get the car steering up the slope, lodging it as it were, on the road. We all got shaken off from our seat, sprang up and then were thrown down back on the seats. In all this halla-baloo we 'discovered' that my brother had put the car up in the first gear. The car got stuck up after giving a jolt. The gear, of course, broke, but we were, by god's grace, narrowly saved from the death-trap.

We, on our way, all the time wondered as to why such things happen which we had never ever dreamt of – things inexplicable!

Thus when you see things happening around you in your day-to-day life, you might be goaded by the thought–

- Why some people despite being so talented and brilliant do not turn out successful! – Why some people despite hard work, do not achieve the necessary results! We find very ordinary looking people with no sign of brilliance on their face or body-language, occupying the high pedestal of success, and brilliant and qualified persons working under these apparently less brilliant people. Why so!

- Why do we become sometimes under-achievers and at other times over-achievers! – Why, of the two persons with exactly similar talent or brilliance, one turns out to be famous while the after remains annonymous! – Why some people even putting in less labour, get more, while the one who has toiled hard does not get his share of success!

- Why does one child get born in a rich family and the other in a poor one! – Why in an accident 18 people out of 20 die, while 2 are saved with no harm caused! – Why do we, sometimes, get a wicket even on a bad ball, and why even a good ball is hit for a six! – Why often people with resources suffer from ill-health and ailments, whereas those who do not have resource enjoy good health, why...!

Questions like these and a thousand others, for want of a better explanation entail only one answer – and that is – Fate or Luck. If we are able to know about our 'fate' or 'luck', every 'why' begets an answer.

Our fate is a reality, and a fact of life, and not a surprise!

Thus if we delve-deep into the things, we might say that all the things that are happening in our life are the ones that are not 'sponsored' from some other points, it is we who are responsible for their origin.

For, there cannot be any smoke without a fire, there can be no effect without a cause. My perception is that if there would not have occurred any event, this life would not have been existing at all. As such whatever is happening, it is happening as a matter of course, happening naturally. What is due to happen has got to happen, we cannot stop it whether we like it or not.

It often happens that we do an act, and then forget all about it. And then when we get the results of the act, they appear to be very strange. We begin to think that whatever is happening is a gift of fate.

Thus we tend to label every event as 'Fate' and tend to get rid of and get disconnected with the matter. Whereas the truth is that whatever happens, or takes place is 'our reality' or our own doing. We cannot evade the reality by giving it the name of fate. Therefore, we should admit, confess and recognise that the fate is nothing but our reality, a reality conceived and created by our own self, and not some surprising thing outside us, not some miracle.

In fact, we do not keep ourselves aware of our karma (duty), instead we engage ourselves with the coincidences of the karma, and think that they are what 'fate' is all about. In other words, we look more to the shadows than to the substance. And in the process we lose sight of the question : why does all this happen to us! The whole thing goes wrong because we miss to find the answer. In order to understand the whole thing, we will have to understand the meaning or concept of fate in its right perspective.

If we look carefully, we come to find that doing some act or not doing it, our involvement with the act alone decides our fate. Or to put it in another way, objective–based intention, or motive at the bottom of our conscience becomes our fate. In other words, our fate is what our 'real intention' is, our real 'mind' is. It is our real motive or mind or intent behind an act that is the deciding factor.

That is precisely the reason why good and honest intention lifts us up and the dishonesty of our intention causes our downfall. Bad intention – intention to deceive – causes our downfall, whereas good intention serves to save us from getting drowned in the dirty waters of misconduct. The intention behind an act formulates our fate, which, in turn, makes our life worthy or unworthy, a success or otherwise.

Readers, just see how the intention serves to operate in a man's life – A certain person had to buy a car. He had enough money with him to buy a car, but he had invested his money for interest-purposes with a Company. The fellow, of course, wanted to have the car but did not want to take out that money and lose the interest. Soon an idea struck him –'Why not I take money from my friend. By this I will be able to save my money and my purpose too will be served. With this intention in mind he went to his friend and made a request for it, saying that it was needed for an emergent purpose. Like a true friend the person helped him out in this hour of need. He bought the car forthwith and he put it up on hire purposes for his own profit.

Encouraged by this, he took yet another money from a relative of his and put this too on interest. He felt very proud of his intelligence in doing all this. He thought he was making profit on all front.

One fine morning when he got up, to his utter dismay, he found his car missing. He felt extremely grieved. In the meanwhile there came a phone call from his friend telling him – 'Yaar, you were lucky that the money I gave to you was timely utilised by you'. In fact the company in which we had thought of investing our money in, has been liquidated. Shock is what he got at the news. He was telling his friend now – 'Oh I too have invested my money into the same bank. Now, how shall I repay such a huge amount to the people?'

The story brings out a big thing, a big fact of life, namely, that no set of circumstances can become what it is, *without our agreeing to it,* without our consent. It is we who make our situations, because fate is not something outside us, some outside agency. It is a part of our inner self. (The kind of consent we give to the fate to grow up like, will decide the kind of circumstances that will develop and come up before us)

Thus fate develops inside us. The extent of its development depends upon how much freedom we allow it in its development. In other words, it is we ourselves who decides and allow it how much to grow. It is we ourselves who let it grow inside us to the extent we want it to grow. So in a way it is we ourselves who dictate fate to produce circumstances. We are the makers of our own fate and our circumstances. We can cause circumstances to be made and can make our own fate.

Dear readers – if our intentions are clear, the forces of Nature will always be ready to support us, but if our intentions are not clear, then nature will not hesitate to weaken us.

By having clean intentions, we can save ourselves from falling into trouble. It is the intentions that are the cause of our being or not being action-persons.

Karma is supreme, Fate gets involved with it.

We generally hold the view bordering on the philosophy that 'Destiny is character' and wish that we sit idle at home and thanks to destiny, may get everything that we wish without ourselves doing anything, without taking any pains. We consider Fate as our slave. And what turns out ultimately is that after a certain time, we leave ourselves at its mercy, doing nothing and expecting that some invisible power will come and fulfill all our wishes and then vanish into nothingness – which in fact is not going to happen.

This is exactly that kind of situation as when we close the nostrils and keep them pressed with our hand, and then vainly expect some gust of fresh air to come and open the nose and enter it.

The hard fact is that as we do the act, so shall we get the reaction. We go on getting the result or the fruit in the proportion or the manner in which we work. The result or the fruit of work is inherent in our Karma already. We cannot separate the two even if like to do so. In other words, the fruit (of work) has to come up. Grow and it will come up; if not today, then tomorrow. It has got to and bound to grow and come up. If we have sown the seeds of ladyfinger, the produce will be ladyfinger alone. It can not happen that the seeds of the ladyfinger result in the production of brinjals. We all know this full well... It is after all such a simple thing!

But if we all know this, then the question arises – despite all this why so much pain, agony, stress, tension, pressures, perversions, disturbances, disallusions and failures in life? – Why?

It appears that we know everything full well, yet tend to pretend that we are not aware of things!

Knowing thoroughly well that by planting an Aak plant, we would be getting a bitter and poisonous fruit, still we plant Aak plant alone and again we expect sweet and juicy pomegranate fruit to come up. We are labouring under a grave misunderstanding and misconception, for, each time we shall be getting Aak fruit only.

To remain pre-occupied, by something which is not done with a right intention, and for this reason to avoid doing something which is right, is the root cause of all evils.

You must be wondering here as to why we happen to evade the right intentions. The answer to this question is – 'because of discrimination' which is a creature of what we call the – 'faculty of discretion'.

Besides those who are a part of our life, there are many others who come in our contact. There is always a certain reason behind their coming in contact with us. But without trying to find out more about them or about the reason or purpose of their coming in contact with us, we start dubbing them in our mind as a friend or enemy, ours or others', black or fair, useful or useless, high or low, rich or poor etc and we start treating them accordingly. In this way, by being influenced by the atmosphere and outside forces around us, we come to treat them in a rather unfair way and by doing so regularly every now and then, we add one more 'unjust action' to our account. In this way this chain goes on continuing and lengthening, which is something that is dangerous for us in future. By indulging in this, again and again, we stray away from the normal course of right intention.

It may be noted that there is nothing there in Nature and its other phenomena that is discriminating vis-a-vis us. Nature gives shelter to all, irrespective of whether we are rich or poor. The rays of the sun do not discriminate between people, they fall equally on all. Water is always eager to quench the thirst of the thirsty whether high or low. The air does not see whether this is ours or it is others. In the same way an ATM machine, or car or a telephone, or other facilities or 'means' – they work for or serve all their users, equally. They do not discriminate between users.

All the discriminations, in fact, are man made. They are Man's inventions. They are the 'mischievous' creations. This discrimination is the root cause behind all our failures in life. It is the attitude that determines the real nature of our character. And our character determines our course of action, that is our deeds, and it is these deeds that are our fate.

Always remember – our Karma (our life of action or deeds) is the supreme most phenomenon, and the dominant force, the fate is included therein. Our Karma is the decider of our success or failures. Karma is the basic source of all our griefs or happiness.

When we are dispassionate in our approach to things and persons, when we have no prejudices or biases, then like Nature, we will not be discriminative in our thoughts and actions, then we will be able to keep ourself off from the wrong actions or deeds and will be able to keep ourselves connected and committed to what is right action, right deed.

Those who care to do the right things need not care for fate. Fate itself prepares for them new pathways of opportunity. This clearly proves the proposition that success does not come on account of fate, it comes by making your fate, yourself. That is why your job, for achieving success, is to work and if you do so, the success–oriented luck will itself be carved out simultaneously, automatically in your favour.

Miracles do not happen, they are made.

"Far away from the madding crowd of culture and civilization. Yunus Khan and his Rural Bank had shown that the poor can make development on their own and thus can change their own life."

- Vide Complement from the Nobel Prize Committee in their address of felicitation for Yunus Khan on the occasion of the 2006 Award Ceremony.

It is often remarked that – 'to work is in our hands, but reward is not thy concern' and is not in our hands.

But the reality is a step farther. Had the above saying been true nobody would have been preoccupied with work, nor would have been detached from work. In fact, to work is in our hands, but no, not only this, *even the result of the work is also in our hand*. For instance, if an ailing person comes to know already that a particular hospital is closed on the particular day, will he go to that hospital then? – No, never

In fact, the theory of Karma is a testimony not of the uncertainty of the results, it is a testimony of the certainty of the result. The Karma theory advises us to remain free from the *tyranny of the pressure of the result*, while we are at work, so that our attention is not distracted from the result, instead it is kept focussed on to the work with the increased chances of better results. But some of our friends put a wrong meaning on the correct and ideal principle of Karma. They misinterpret it, perhaps because their own attention is not on action and better performance, but on the result of the action.

Those who say that there is nothing that is in your hands, are in fact people having some vested interests. They work to their profit, not yours. Because they know that the moment others came to know this, who would go to them for advice?

These days our friends are more particular, more concerned about their future, wishing it to be bright. This is the reason that the profession of fortune-telling has caught on. Everybody is after his future to be bright and shining. If any future-teller astrologer could make your future bright, why has he not been able to brighten his own future? – Of course, this is possible that some such professional might guide you into showing the correct way. But again – who is going to use that way?

At this point of our life, whatever situation, good or bad, is there, it is a precipitation of our past coincidences. This is the reason why the coincidences of the past cut across the present successes. Until and unless we are able to liberate ourselves from these past coincidences, we will not be able to reach out to the new successes.

Then, can we be liberated from our cumulative coincidences? – The answer to this question is – 'Yes, we can.'

We can reduce the effect of the cumulative coincidences by reformatory deeds. At the same time we can associate ourselves with purposeful and meaningful objectives and get rid of the cumulative coincidences.

We have to understand this point with due seriousness. Supposing somebody comes out of his house and wants to go up to the crossing for buying vegetables. A certain dog sees him in the way out there and barks at him loudly. Angered at this, the man picks up a piece of stone and cruelly throws it to hit the creature. Groaning with agony of the pain caused by the hurt the dog runs away from the place. Now the event of hitting the dog before buying the vegetables becomes a past event for him. To be redeemed from stigma of the act of hitting the dog, has already become, for the man, a part of his fate now.

Supposing good sense comes to him and he feels sorry for what he had done. Now he may, if he likes, manage to arrange a proper treatment for the dog. By doing so he can mitigate the effect of his Karma or the deed. Again he can further liberate himself from this stigma by taking up the cause of taking care of the helpless animals whenever possible and of providing them safety and better living conditions. But then as against all this, if he starts hitting the dogs cruelly at the very sight of them, the very next day, God save such a soul from falling into the well of sins and be doomed!

Nature gives us exactly what we want. It does not miss to do so. This is the Nature's 'Law of Giving'. We can get something from Nature provided we follow the Laws of Nature.

The one straight mode of getting quick and fruitful result of our Karmas is to sow, in the present, the seeds of good Karmas or right action and then to continue to do so regularly and certainly on every day of our life. We will find that, by and by, the cumulative Karmas will have been dealt with and considered fully on their merits and we will go on getting nearer our real fate, and a moment will come when all our debts will have been cleared off, and we will get the result of our present Karmas forthwith, hand to hand. Encouraged by this, we will adopt the course of good deeds every time. This will raise our graph of attainments high – which, in fact, would be the real, genuine success. – By living in the constant company of pure feelings, we can be real fortunate guys.

For one who keeps actively working for success, being successful will be natural, and for one who keeps standing watching it, the same success would be a miracle. This apart, no success or venture for success is beyond man's reach, man's knowledge and power.

Therefore we are tempted to say that, in fact, no miracle ever 'happens', it is done or caused by forces of knowledge and power that we possess.

It is not our job to wait for miracles. On the other hand, we are supposed to work for miracles. For, we can change our fate only by keeping working in the right earnest. And so *this* is the time – *now is the time which is most appropriate for the fine flowering of our fortune.*

Come, let us espouse those intentions, working for which, we may become the real fortunate creatures, so that with the success of our intentions, our fortune may keep shining brighter, and the stream of success in our life may keep ever running on...

Substance...

Pay attention to the following points :-

- Life is full of strange happenings, and as such I shall keep on getting thrilled with its amazing strangeness or peculiarities.
- A question will often arise while analysing the happenings in my life – Why does it so happen? I shall hunt out the answer and then shall cultivate a correct attitude towards life.
- The cause behind every happening that transpires in my life is 'I' myself, and is nobody else.
- There is a long series of events which have been taking place in my life since long and to every chain thereof a link has been present there. This link has been provided by me. I have created this link. In other words, whatever things are going to happen today, are the result of my own previous happenings.
- Whatever is happening is happening in the natural course. I shall accept its naturalness, and I shall not blame anybody for this.
- My fate is my reality. Recognising this reality I shall carve out my (good) intentions and to realise these intentions, I shall create favourable and profitable circumstances.
- I shall sow the seeds of my life of action, and remaining active in my world of work, I shall brighten my fate.
- Behind the coming of every person in my life there has always been a certain cause. Keeping in mind these causes, I shall treat everybody well.
- I shall take to my life of action, despite my basic quality of innocence. Thereby I shall keep myself connected to right action or good deeds rather than to wrong action or bad deeds.
- Just as to act lies in my power, similarly it lies in my power, to reap its results. Keeping this attitude, I shall keep trying out my powers and strengths.
- I shall 'currently' pay my 'attention' specifically to good deeds, keeping unmindful of their results. By doing so, I shall really become the author of my destiny.

The Present Alone is Our Reality...
It is eternal... It is its own reason...

**Either we are too deeply sunk into the past, or else,
too pre-occupied with or concerned for the future**

Two close friends set out to spend a holiday at some nice spot of natural scenic beauty. When they reached there they were taken in by the sheer beauty of the sight around. It was a feast for the eye. Nature itself appeared to be having a gala time. The first friend drawing the other friend's attention towards the natural scenery, commented that the ice-clad mountain peaks were looking enchanting – 'The thick cluster of trees standing magnificently amidst the surroundings, one feels like wandering aimlessly in these valleys with no care on the mind, one feels like never leaving this place and wishing to get belonged to it' – This is how this friend reacted at the enchanting scenic beauty of the place.

On the other hand, the second friend was caught in a chain of home-thoughts:- 'Whether Rahul went to school or not? His mummy is a late-riser – whether she could manage to send Rahul to school in time? And that neighbor of mine Sohanlal, who had picked a quarrel with me just about the time I was leaving... what happened thereafter...?' This friend was too preoccupied with all these home-thoughts.

The first friend ignoring his friend's utterances, changed the point and suggested that they ought to get up early and enjoy the delightful and refreshing morning walk, besides going up a high hill-peak and enjoy the scenic beauty around from the next day onwards'. With these words he looked at his companion with quite some eagerness.

But, again, his friend was being haunted by all sorts of worries. He stated that by the time he reached back, files of office work may have turn into a big pile and that unfortunately, his General Manager's visit was also due about the same time. Moreover he would have to go his village immediately thereafter, as his brother's marriage preparations were pending to be completed. These and many other worries had been occupying his mind.

The first fellow however did not give up. Taking his friend's hand in his own he reacted rather angrily, – "Oh my dear, where are you? Do you know that you are holidaying with me out here in this beautiful place. Why can't you enjoy these precious moments? Why all this unwanted cribbing?"

This piece of scolding kind-of alerted the second friend and he became a bit more normal. Catching sight of a water-fall the two souls got engrossed in enjoying the amazing sight and pleasing sounds of the music of the fall of the water from the hills.

The point to ponder here is :- what is present before us is overpowered by the thoughts that either belong to or pertain to the past, or are those that are addressed to the worries or concerns of the future. In other words, often despite being in the present, we tend to lose our contact with it, 'it' here meaning the present moment; the result is that what should not be, comes to happen, and what should be or ought to be, does not happen. –What a paradox! What irony!

It is so, not because 'time' does not help us, but because we do not cooperate with 'time'. Our mind gets occupied with the particular 'time' we are thinking of. Therefore, we should first take care to know what is required of us at the particular moment in question. In other words, we should be cautious enough to know what we are supposed to do at that moment. As soon as we address ourselves to the aim or our objective, our thoughts would return to the present.

Concentration helps us in sticking to the present

Thoughts keep on coming to or going from our mind all the time. These thoughts pertain to things which we have already been done or things which are called for to be done by us in the coming time. This is a natural phenomenon and there is nothing wrong in it and nothing to worry about. But the fact or the truth remains that we tend to be preoccupied with the past or the future thoughts, and in the process we lose our contact with or awareness of the present time.

Our job is not to get unwantedly worried over these thoughts. Instead, our job is to take our mind away from unwanted thoughts. We, instead, make ourselves stick to our objective or our principal aim, that is, we should keep stuck to our present situation and keep ourselves committed to the 'present', and refuse to be influenced by ideas or thoughts which essentially relate to the past or future.

When, concentrating on one single target, our thinking power does not get restricted. In fact, it becomes stronger and wider in range and we are able to address ourselves to our objective with a sharper intellect and are able to realise them in a more reassured manner of thought. This is the miracle of what is known as 'concentration'. Concentration lends dynamism to the purposeful, productive thoughts, and leaves alone the thoughts which have no objective, which are not productive or purposeful.

When we are in concentration, we look to our thoughts dispassionately, objectively like an independent witness. In such a state of mind we come to judge our thoughts with full awareness on our part, just as we see all other things in the day-to-day life, and thus we are able to sift the productive thoughts from those that are not useful. In this process we allow the useless thoughts to be passed over and do not let ourselves be prone to them, that is, we do not entertain them, and instead, let them pass by. We are not influenced by such thoughts, nor do we apply our mind and so concentration does not get disturbed if we are addressing ourselves to one single objective.

But it *does* get disturbed if we are drawn to more objectives than one. For instance, while driving a vehicle your main work is to drive the vehicle. But while driving your mind entertains certain other extraneous thoughts and gets busy with them, your concentration is bound to be get affected and is sure to get strayed away, and in a situation like this, there are chances of an accident taking place. The moral is that at one given point of time we cannot remain in different times – present, past and future.

However, many of our more adventurous friends attempting miracles do tend to address themselves to past and future times along with their present task, with the result that they keep their activities floating and alternating between the imagined past and future, and despite belonging to the 'present' time they are not able to put their foot on it. It is not rather ironical? Certainly, it is.

Neither in past nor in the 'future' lies the success, it lies only in the 'present'

The moments that are gone by are really gone. And the moment that has not yet come, really has not come. What is the point, then, in thinking about it when what in fact you come to get is unnecessary mental tension, frustration, excitement, disappointment etc.

Those who carry on their minds a big bundle of memories of old things, they are not able to get away from them in the coming times. They keep clung on to their mind unnecessarily. We are neither able to come out of the past, nor are we able to apprehend the future moments. For, until we leave the past, there is no room for the present to occupy. It is all a matter of space. Suppose, you are holding a bucket in one hand and you are required to place a picture frame on the table, you will pick up the picture frame but not until you have emptied your hands of the bucket. As soon as you have placed the bucket down on the floor, the picture-frame will find place for it automatically.

Again, often we begin to take up on our head the burden of a task the time for doing of which is yet to come. We go on thinking about it repeatedly and make our mind heavy with the burden of the thoughts much in advance. This is wholly unnecessary. Supposing some task has to be done at 5 PM and we start thinking of or worrying about it since morning itself. The result is that by the time, the time for doing that work comes, we are already too tired mentally to tackle it properly and do it thoroughly. Also with a heavy and disturbed mind the chances are that we will not be able to do justice to all those tasks which have preceded the 5 PM-work. And then there are chances that there may have been some other development or change in the programme. Thus we lose ourselves in the two unreal worlds – the past and the future.

This is not living with the time, but is like falling a prey to the times.

It is a different matter to plan things for the future on basis of the past-time experiences, but it is quite another to create clouds of tensions in the mind, by 'worrying' about things. Planning or thinking will make our future smooth, while 'just worrying about' will cause tensions which is bad for our work as well as for the health of our mind.

Just as we have the ability of forgetting things, similarly we possess the guts to remember things too. By resorting to doing the exercise of remembering, we can train our mind in the matter of remembering or forgetting. So if we want to remember things apply the success-ideas and if we wish to forget something apply the failure-ideas as discussed in this book. However, all said and done, ultimately our memory will be retaining only success-ideas.

Agreed, for example, that we can work for 10 hours a day, but to think or assume that we could do the work of 10 hours just in the first hour itself, would it be right? —Perhaps not, and therefore, there is no point in mixing the work of the 1st hour with that of the rest 9 hours.

Wisdom, therefore lies in the fact that whatever work is in hand at the moment, must occupy our mind and not some other thing. This will make our work more joyful. For, just as one particular work is over, we could easily switch over to the next work, and similarly from the next onto the next and so on. In this way, we come to have a sense of satisfaction that the work is getting completed. This would enhance our confidence, lessen our worry because of the coverage of the pending work. All this because we will be going on to deal with the present, and in the process we will go on getting rid of the past and the future, as all the time the present will be before us occupying the central stage.

We are thus in a position to conclude that the present is the real reality and it is eternal and has a scientific or rational philosophy behind it.

Present alone is reality

If somebody is asked – 'How are you? How is your work going on?' etc, mostly the answer we get is like this – It will become OK as soon as my child's studies are over. – Next meeting the same question and the answer is – 'Fine, but how I wish, first we got a good girl for him – then... Next time, again and the same question and the answer this time too - 'Oh yes all well but just one wish – my child gets satisfactorily married... Similar encounter again, the same question and the answer again would be – 'Well but just only one wish – my son begets a child...' Now you may notice thus that all the time we tend to keep *running after wishes*. While we are all the time thinking of some 'future' thing, we just ignore the present moment we are in. We always tend to look forward to some future event for our happiness; we keep all the time thinking in terms of future happiness and success, and not in the present and present success. We ignore the present moment and are keen on success at some future time.

This is something like this, namely, that while we are living in the year 2007, we are more worried about success we expect to get in the year 2009.

Or else we tend to look back engaging ourselves with scanning of some past success, namely the successes of 2005 or 2006 and then we wish to see these successes to be repeated. And this repetition may not occur at all. It may not take place because we are just indulging in a hypothetical act or in wishful thinking.

Dear readers, it is clear from the above examples that we are wasting our present moments for a future moment, which is just an imaginary exercise, as it may not come to happen at all. Every day we wake up to a new 'present' and not to a present that is already gone. Something can happen only at the time we are really 'doing' something. It can not happen either before or after that moment.

Can it happen that you might drink the pineapple-shake at 10'O clock in the morning and you may get the energy from it at 10'O clock in the night. The energy that you get is at the time you have drunk the pineapple shake. Again it cannot happen that you have taken mango shake on the Wednesday and you expect the energy from it on the Monday that has gone by. Both these possibilities are not viable to take place. That's why what is real is not the moment gone by or the moment that is yet to come. What is real, then, is the 'present' -the present moment, which should not be allowed to be slipped, by uneventfully and unproductively. Apprehend this moment, as this, out here, is the grass-root reality.

It is sad that we have all this while engaged ourselves with the task of explaining the infinite possibilities of life in terms of pleasure. By doing so we are be-littling the vastness of life. We have reduced happiness to a set of celebrations and festivals etc. and we are 'supposed to be' happy while we are celebrating these festivals, functions or occasions. On the rest of the days we are left to grapple with the failures and sorrows of life.

What we should in fact, realise is that happinesses do not need to be 'reserved' in any manner, we cannot confine happiness to or reserve it for a few occasions, festivals etc. As such happiness does not know any reservation. What it requires is success. When we work with a free mind for success, happiness automatically follows. It is then that we realise that we are in the midst of the present.

Joy lies in doing something for success. So we will be in the 'present' only when we are really working for our success. And when this is the situation, joy and happinesses would automatically follow. It is in such a state that we begin to feel we are there in the present.

All the principles of science reflect the present form of Nature. For instance, when the great scientist Newton saw the apple fall from the tree, Newton's attention went to the present time and as a live witness to this event wherein he deduced the principle : 'Law of Gravitation'. In fact he became active and 'involved with the moment' or let us say he 'observed and captured that moment', and as such we might say that he had captured the 'present' time and had opened significantly new vistas of knowledge for us. Nature, as we already know, has only one relevant face for us and that is its present face, not a past, nor a future face.

In fact, the past and the future are not the realities of time. They are just reckoners of time. The 'present' is the real reality of time, the real time. It is eternal. It has its own reason, and therefore, it is a scientific phenomenon. In this sense it is 'science' itself. The present moment is eternal, steadfast, and permanent, inviolable and unchangeable.

In fact, happiness or joy is a passing moment a passing phenomenon. It can neither be tied down, nor be stopped. It cannot be apprehended or caught by the collar. It is like the oxygen that goes inside our body when we breath in and comes out when the air is exhaled. Every breath we take reminds us that we are full of life yet. And this realisation showing that we are full of life, serves as a reminder that we are 'live and kicking' even for our future successes. Success is needed for the happiness that every moment, involves – it is needed always, continuously, regularly, and perpetually... in fact, till the life exists.

Be proactive with every coming moment because it is not going to stay with you for long. It is destined to go. Be active with each moment, so that you may discover in it and achieve, new successes. And the next moment again has the promise of success. Encash it. Do not keep, in respect of your work, an attitude of monotony. Do not think that you are doing the same work that you did yesterday. Behave everyday with your work in such a manner that it may sound a new work. This will give you a refreshing feeling and add value to that work by using your intellect as well as imagination. The work may be the same old type, but you should behave with your work in such a manner that even you yourself may feel that it is some new kind of work. This will save you from burden of monotony. When we use our own discretion to refine or redefine our present, the day that has gone past, that is, yesterday, gets lost in oblivion and 'tomorrows' that go on coming, keep on being better... This is really 'progress'.

By becoming progressive, we can see such of 'prosperities' or wealth in reality, the dreams whereof we see everyday. We shall talk about those items of wealth (prosperities) in detail in the second part of this book.

For the time being, however, we have to see that the ideal situations that we have been waiting for, have not yet come. non are they likely to even come in future. As such whatever most favourable situation is there, it is there in the 'present' time, in the present moment, in the 'present' alone. If we are happy at this time, we are really happy. Having seen all such things, we should by now, have come to the conclusion of realising that – *every moment is a moment of joy, moment of happiness.*

Let us now turn to considering those things which are full with the promise of success, so that we might turn them into action and be successful, as also that we might 'feel good' and say – 'I am extremely happy at the moment' – and then on being encouraged thereby, we might work and remain active with redoubled energy and zeal...

Substance...

Pay attention to the following points :-

- Life lies before me, full with its freshness to the brim. I shall live with it and shall enjoy the maximum that it offers.
- I shall see to it as to what I have to do at a given point of time. By this I shall be able to come back to the present moment and shall resume doing what I am supposed to do at present and shall keep on doing it as well.
- I shall keep a discriminating eye on my thoughts. I shall keep in mind only useful thoughts, letting others to be out of it. By doing so I will be able to live away from the past or future and shall keep committed to the present.
- I shall direct my abilities to a particular area with full concentration, and in this way shall be able to exploit them to their maximum.
- I shall not keep on my mind the burden of (the thoughts of) the past or of future and shall keep myself concerned with and concentrated on the present action. I shall be keeping my peace of mind thereby.
- Just as I have the power of forgetting with me, in the same manner, I have got with me the power of remembering. By making adequate use of this power, I shall conserve the thoughts of success and shall let the stream of these thought run through the course of time.
- I shall be doing only one work at a time and shall not mix with it the other tasks. In this way my tasks shall be getting accomplished one after another in a quick succession.
- I shall not give up today's delight for the unsure joy of tomorrow. By doing so I shall be living each day of my life in its own fullness and richness.
- I shall treat the coming events or moments as though they are meant to pass off soon. In this way I shall be living each moment with a new zeal of its own and thereby make my life sweet with the fragrance of this new zeal around.
- I shall turn the situations in my favour whatever circumstances I may have been in and at the same time I shall consciously let myself nurse the feeling that – I am extremely happy.

About the Author

Being interested in a broader vision of human welfare and happiness, based on optimum self-growth of individuals, Mr. Parvat Singh has written a lot on the subject. His homely style has won him a wide readership. He is living with his family at Jodhpur (Rajasthan) India.